W9-DHK-537

SMALL CHRISTIAN COMMUNITIES

SMALL CHRISTIAN COMMUNITIES

Imagining Future Church

Robert S. Pelton, C.S.C., Editor

Copyright 1997 by
University of Notre Dame Press
Notre Dame, IN 46556
All Rights Reserved
Manufactured in the United States of America

Library of Congress Cataloging-in-Publication Data

Small Christian communities : imagining future church / Robert S.
    Pelton, editor.
        p.   cm.
    Collection of essays presented at the third Notre Dame
International Theological Consultation on Small Christian
Communities, held in 1996 at the University of Notre Dame.
    Includes bibliographical references.
    ISBN 0-268-01761-1 (pa. : alk. paper)
    1. Christian communities—Catholic Church—Congresses.
2. Catholic Church—Developing countries—Congresses.   3. Small
groups—Congresses.   I. Pelton, Robert S., 1921–   .   II. Notre
Dame International Theological Consultation on Small Christian
Communities (3rd : 1996 : University of Notre Dame)
BX2347.7.S53   1997
262'.26—dc21   97-34882
                                                                CIP

∞The paper used in this publication meets the minimum requirements
of the American National Standard for Information Sciences—
Permanence of Paper for Printed Library Materials, ANSI Z39.48-1984.

CONTENTS

PREFACE

In the late sixties the Chilean Catholic Church gave official and strong impetus to the formation of small Christian communities. Eight years of pastoral service with some of these communities, together with occasional visits to similarly constituted Christian base communities in Brazil, convinced me that they had the potential to give flesh to the biblical image of the Church as the people of God—a concept that was valued so highly in the Second Vatican Council.

Today these communities are present throughout the world. They flourished in the 1970s and subsequently some have matured, while others have faded away. Mistakes have been made, and in some cases corrected, leading to greater growth. On occasion there has been an overly optimistic perception of the influence of the communities. While they are very attractive, they are a clear minority in the Church. However, the possibility of their influence for a deeper living out of the theology of Church may be stronger than it appears. This is what we searched for in the 1996 Notre Dame International Theological Consultation on Small Christian Communities.

One of the research themes of Notre Dame's Helen Kellogg Institute for International Studies, founded in 1982 and now internationally recognized as one of the leading centers of Latin American studies, is small Christian communities. These communities were a major focus of debate at the 1982 Kellogg conference on "The Catholic Church in Latin America." Seven years later Kellogg co-hosted a related international conference at Notre Dame, "Medellín and Puebla: Their Impact on the Church and Society," which explored the effects on the Latin American and U.S. Churches, of the historic 1968 and 1979 meetings of the Latin American Bishops Conference (CELAM). At Medellín the bishops blessed these communities. At Puebla the bishops affirmed them while insisting upon their ecclesial identity. The Santo Domingo meeting (1992) continued to support these communities.

LANACC (Latin American/North American Church Concerns) of the Kellogg Institute was founded in 1985. It promotes a pastoral bond between the Churches of the Americas. This has been in good part a mission of information, interpreting the Catholicism of Latin America to that of its fellow communicants of the north by the publication of Church documents, by a lecture series such as that dedicated to the memory of Archbishop Romero, and by special conferences such as those about the small Christian communities (SCCs). Thus, in 1990 LANACC sponsored a consultation which brought together those organizations which promote these communities. These groups are the National Alliance of Parishes, which promotes the restructuring of parishes into small communities; the North American Forum for Small Christian Communities, which is composed of diocesan directors of small communities; and Buena Vista, which represents grass-roots small communities who do not necessarily pertain to Church structures. These organizations formed a joint task force at Notre Dame in 1991 in order to sponsor occasional national convocations.

In 1991 an International Consultation on Small Communities was held at the University. This placed emphasis upon comparing pastoral experiences. The 1996 meeting provided the opportunity to delve more deeply into those theological dimensions of small communities that may influence our Church as we enter a new millennium. In his introductory essay Robert O'Gorman of Loyola University in Chicago spells out the theological methodology we employed. This consultation took place in the context of a series of continental synods of bishops: the African synod in 1994; the synod for America in 1997; and the synod for Asia scheduled for 1998. Small Christian communities have played a prominent role in the discussion and documentation of all of these synods.

As Bernard Lee puts it: "There is no more central question than what kind of community the Church needs to be today, faithful to its origins and interdependently interactive in the world in which it lives."[1] It is our sincere hope that the fruits of this Notre Dame Consultation will contribute to the response to this question.

Robert S. Pelton, C.S.C.

Note

1. Bernard J. Lee, *The Future Church of 140 B.C.E.* (New York: Crossroad Herder, 1995), p. 160.

ACKNOWLEDGMENTS

I am grateful to James R. Langford, director, University of Notre Dame Press; and Ann Rice, executive editor, Notre Dame Press, for their expert assistance in preparing this manuscript for publication; and to Notre Dame's Helen Kellogg Institute for International Studies for scholarly support.

THEOLOGICAL METHODOLOGY AS INCARNATED IN SMALL CHRISTIAN COMMUNITIES

An Introduction

Robert O'Gorman

"The concern for 'method' . . . has, in many respects, taken center stage in our post-modern religious world" writes Barbara Fleisher.[1] "[T]he major methodological shift that has occurred in this century is toward theological inquiry that grounds itself in the human experience of the persons and communities doing theology, a development rooted in the 'turn to the subject' initiated by theologians like Karl Rahner and Bernard Lonergan."

The marriage between human experience and classical religious language in the theological enterprise has birthed a new mode of doing theology, termed practical, praxic, or contextual theology.[2] Unlike the older meaning attached to "practical theology" as the "applied discipline" flowing from the theory found in the classical theological specialties, practical theology as a new approach to doing theology calls upon communities to reflect upon interpretations of their cultural realities in conversation with interpretations of the Christian tradition (texts, symbols, story, and vision), with a focus on the question of what kind of world we should be creating together as agents in history.[3]

The Theological Consultation on Small Christian Communities had both an explicit concern for and implicit expression of method. This chapter will reflect on the operative methodology of this consultation and how it added to our experience of this vital issue of theological method.

This event was planned as a *consultation* on the development of church as small community. It intended to take the international and ecumenical *experience* of people who in the past thirty years have participated in the birth of church as small community and reflect on two theological themes of this development: christology and ecclesiology. Specifically, two guiding questions emerged: "How is an understanding of Christ informed by this development in the body of Christ?" and, "How is the development of church as small community both faithful to the call to be church as well as an unfolding of that tradition?"

The context of this event is essential to its method. It was the third such gathering on small communities of this decade, all sponsored by Notre Dame's Latin American/North American Church Concerns (LANACC) under the direction of Rev. Robert S. Pelton, C.S.C. This event included collaboration with the Institute of Pastoral Studies at Loyola University, Chicago, and the Maryknoll Center for Mission Research, Maryknoll, N.Y.

For more than two years a small group met regularly to plan the event. Their methodological watch words were *desde abajo,* or as it is said in bluegrass country "keep it close to the ground." The work of the people has to be the base of our reflection. This consultation was committed to participatory theological research in order to organize faith communities for mission, not merely to produce a text. *El Projecto,* the "project" of the Notre Dame Consultation intended to articulate and affect the reality of the new sense of church for the people.[4]

The planners needed to give direction to particular avenues of reflection for two broad topics: emerging christology and emerging ecclesiology. They began to do that methodologically by asking Sobrino's question: "Where does one find the reality of Christ?" This question contrasts "a christology that is forced" from one that is "from below."[5] In addition they engaged further cutting-edge questions: How does the experience of women as actors in church as small community give us new insight into methodical questions? What are the leading themes in christology? What is the relationship of small communities with the institution? Will small communities be so homogeneous that they may not represent the *sensus fidelium* and thus may disconnect from the tradition?

The dynamic of this consultation involved interaction among scholars, pastoral leaders, and people from small Christian communities, using the structure of small groups that stayed together for four days. The schedule for the first two days was the same: in the mornings christology and ecclesiology, respectively, were explored through the presentation of informational papers; in the afternoons small groups met to bring forth insights, ask questions, and articulate concerns; in the evenings a circle of all participants shared insights, questions, and concerns. The third day was dedicated to the preparation and integration of draft summaries. Day four was a plenary session for developing a concluding articulation.

Forty-five people from five continents and eleven countries drew from their experience in church as small community. They described just how their own understanding of Jesus and the church had developed. The experiences of participating bishops, theologians, faith community organizers, and group members were equal in voice.

In summary, this consultation hoped to mine the experience of small communities, the reflections of theologians, and the pastoral guidance of designated church leaders in order to identify emerging directions in christology and ecclesiology.

The Method of the Consultation

In its methodological framework this consultation embraced the metaphor of dance through four movements: (1) indwelling, (2) inquisitiveness, (3) imagining, and (4) inscription.[6] *Indwelling* calls the participants to an interior open-minded disposition to questions and discussions of christology and ecclesiology. *Inquisitiveness* highlights their reception to personal and small group interactions. *Imagining* begins the responsive task of capturing the images arising from their experiences and discussions: images from Scripture, church tradition, or life experiences. *Inscription* captures the responsive task of writing and editing the consultation's articulation for sharing with the wider church and theological community.

Day One

Indwelling

Indwelling began on the opening evening with a social gathering and dinner after which the participants were divided into eight small groups representing the diversity of the consultation. In the first session participants began to share life experiences, as well as their hopes and expectations for this meeting, and began to form a consultation community. Each of the forty-five participants had personal experience of small Christian community. Participants wrote the name of their home group on a poster that hung in the plenary meeting hall all week long. This first act of participants identifying their communities grounded the reflections of the week.

Indwelling continued the next morning at the first session with information, "Emerging Christologies of SCCs" by Monika Hellwig, a theologian from the United States. She reviewed how the early church talked about Jesus from their experience of him in their midst and how they experienced his presence after he was gone. She emphasized that this experience came from the whole of the people. Hellwig outlined how later descriptions of Jesus were articulated by a narrower and narrower community of people—monastics and then scholastics—resulting in systematic descriptions of who the Christ is. These descriptions were articulated in language further and further distant from the ordinary lives of ordinary people.

Hellwig concluded that only when people start with the Scriptures and immediately connect this Jesus to their experience does christology from below happen. She pointed out this was a return to true discipleship—to be formed not by a set rule but by a "quest" for Jesus. The key achievement of the laity was gaining the courage to share their experience and insights from their quest even though they were different from those offered by many theologians.

In summary, the impact of this from-below christology is a critique of the Constantinian Christ as "super emperor," a critique of a divinity of Christ that excludes his humanity, and of a christology that emphasizes passion over compassion. It is a critique of the Christ of the colonial outreach that guarantees the status quo and a passive humanity that relegates decision making to divinity. Christology from below promotes an active sense of redemption. It manifests a way to change thinking about grace and empowers people to see, judge, and act, an empowerment that is expressed by relationships in community. This christology produces a fierce revolutionary action for change, threatens verbal orthodoxy, and prompts the church to change.

After having an opportunity to ask clarifying questions, the group spent a few moments in silence dwelling with the words spoken. Participants were invited to jot down words or phrases that stayed with them. Indwelling continued with the presentations of formal respondents, followed by time for questions and discussion in plenary session.

Alywood Shorter, a seminary professor from Nairobi, spoke from an East African perspective in which poverty is seen as evil and Scripture reflection is concrete, often with dramatizations. Church is *family* of God. The human Jesus is an elder brother. God is ultimate ancestor. Jesus' compassion, his activity as healer, and his care for the sick and Jesus as neighbor are key christological interpretations. For East Africa the cross is essential in its christology. It is a sign of contradiction. East Africa's christological elaborations are probably less revolutionary than those of Latin America. They would tend to be more pastoral than political.

Barbara Howard, animator of a small Christian community in Colorado, U.S.A., noted small communities discover Jesus in Scripture. They understand Jesus as passionately involved in lives of real people. The reign of God in Jesus is now. U.S. small Christian communities face the evils of individualism and consumerism more than that of injustice.

Inquisitiveness

The consultation moved to questions of clarification and general response. The group as a whole, in the spirit of 'consulting the faithful in matters of doctrine,' responded to the questions:

In your experience with small Christian communities, what resonated from the presentation and reactions?

What themes from these presentations on christology are staying with you?

What challenge/connection do these presentations make to
your experience in an SCC?

What questions are there for the wider church?

Samples of responses:

Christology is lived out in mutual aid to the needy, visiting the
sick.

Christological discussions should be relations of the heart and
concluded with the "handshake of peace." We need to learn
from the Quakers in regard to resolving christological conflicts.

The cross is a central symbol. It cannot be considered in isolation from the Gospel.

An East African spoke of christology and interfaith dialogue,
expressing the appreciation of other "mediators." This is beginning christology with a large vision. Knowing our own
standpoint is crucial.

Imagining

After the presentation, responses, and reactions the consultation
began its responsive task. Participants were divided into groups of
six. Each group shared images of Jesus arising from experience in
small communities. Images from Scripture, Church tradition and/or
life experience surfaced which spoke to the challenge SCCs offer for
the future in relation to present understandings of christology.
These images were recorded on newsprint and posted in the plenary
meeting room.

What became clear was that knowledge of Jesus needs to pre-
cede understanding of church:

Jesus has to form our idea of church and not vice versa.

The reign of God is first.

Ecclesiology must come from christology.

Jesus is for everyone because he is one of us, not solely a high
priest.

The reign is social and political; SCCs always relate the reign to community.

Inscription

Time was given to view the small groups' images on the posted newsprint sheets. The consultation's first attempt at inscribing an emerging christology of the SCCs had begun. In a plenary session the facilitator posed questions:

What impressions/insights do you carry away from this first day?
Do we have any common threads here?

Responses were recorded from this discussion on newsprint for the benefit of the writing team.

Day Two

The second day the consultation repeated the process of the "dance" steps of (1) indwelling, (2) inquisitiveness (3) imagining and (4) inscription.

Indwelling

Indwelling continued at the first session with the presentation of "Uncanny Grace: Christian Communities and the Survival of Hope" by U.S./Peruvian theologian Curt Cadorette, M.M., who distinguished two different societies from which small groups come: the "developed" and the "developing." He called the first "intentional" and the second "base" communities. The communities formed in the developed world focus on mutual support; those in the developing world focus on social action. These latter groups are people with no social, political, or economic power. Their reason for coming together as church is to respond to the conditions under which they are held by the elites of their society. These communities then are subversive. Their focus is on the "reign of God" and how close or far away it is in their society.

In intentional communities members are "more a part of the problem than the solution." Their separation from the oppression practiced in their society is less distinct than in the base communities. These communities do not contrast with the direction of their society, as happens with the base communities.

The process of developing ideal small community as church is a combination of developing inner life, i.e., interpersonal bonds for mutual support and outer life, i.e., studying critically the signs of the times as we engage Jesus' mission for the reign of God. As an "ideal community," a corporate identity or personality develops and an alternate vision of society emerges.

Connection of small communities to larger diverse communities of the Church is important because experience and analysis in communities that develop into "sectarian" communities is fatal. Cadorette's conclusion on ecclesiology is that the small community is the Church in embryo.

Respondents included both a U.S. theologian and a pastoral agent from Bolivia:

Catherine Nerney, S.S.J., of Philadelphia, noted that Vatican II retrieved "communion" from the patristic period. In addressing the church, *Gaudium et Spes* pointed to the joy, hopes, grief, anxieties, especially of the poor. The church cannot remove itself from the world God so loves. In the world today the church is the reconciling agent of the world's brokenness. The church is those who refuse to believe what the "experts" tell us is the fate of the world.

The SCCs are a concrete realization of *communion*. Communion values are mutual trust, mutual respect, listening to others, extending forgiveness, new behaviors, hospitality, and reconciling divisions.

Alicia Butkiewicz of Cochabamba, Bolivia, claimed SCCs do not emerge by themselves. They need a convocation. In Bolivia, the bishops called the church as small community into being, at the base— with the poor.

The SCC is creating new structures of leadership, leaving ones no longer needed. Now leaders must work as a team, on all levels, to empower people as equals, to emphasize relationships, abandoning competing ways to work. What is now important is who one is, not what one has. The poor have "nothing"; women are the worst off.

Inquisitiveness

The consultation again moved to a plenary session with questions of clarifications and general response. The group as a whole responded to the questions:

Share a significant experience of church from your SCC (its story) addressed in the theme of the presentation on ecclesiology.

What connections are there to the presentation on christology?

What challenge/connection does this presentation make to your experience in SCCs?

What questions does it raise for the wider church?

Some sample responses:

The SCC is a matrix for enculturation.

Enculturation is a value, but how much diversity can be tolerated?

The need to critique the broader church is crucial since Eurocentricism continues. There is no sense of newness.

Our structures are collapsing.

The need is for bridge-builders—to distinguish people in structures from the structures.

Imagining

Participants again joined their small group. Each group shared images of church arising from experience in small communities that spoke to the challenge that the SCCs hold for the future in relation to their understandings of ecclesiology. Again, they captured these on newsprint and posted them in the plenary meeting room.

In the small group discussions people shared different experiences of the church as small groups: a funeral celebration for a member of a twenty-five-year-old community; a banquet experience with street women who are dying.

The following are samples of reflection that emerged:

The focus has to move away from church as institution to church as small community.

We must confess our sins of "ecclesiolatry."

How are the SCCs welcoming diversity into the small groups?
We must judge them in light of the reign of God.

Being church when you are part of a privileged group is more difficult. There is the need for a social analysis of privilege.

Sectarian communities are fatal.

One key problem is that we see the "parish" as the only perspective.

The SCC is the embryo of church, not a "part" of church.

The experience of the small group raises the issue of the celebration of the Eucharist. This is the central act of worship.
There is a crisis: the importance of the Eucharist and the lack of celebrants.

The image of church from one discussion was that of the potluck supper where everyone has a place. Another image was from pyramid to circle: a new way of being church.

Inscription

Newsprint sheets again were posted and time was given to view images from the small groups. In plenary session the facilitator asked:

What impressions/insights do you carry away from this second day?

Do we have any common threads here?"

Responses were again recorded on newsprint for the benefit of the writing team. At the conclusion of this second day a summary outline was prepared and distributed by the writing team. Participants were invited to "dwell" with it overnight.

Day Three: Caucuses

The third day a different form of gathering happened: geographic area "caucuses"—one Latin American, one Asian, one African and four U.S.—discussed the following questions to bring a report back to the plenary group:

What are some critical issues your local church is facing as it
   moves to the future?
Given what we have discussed thus far and the summary document, are there issues or questions for your local church that
   have not yet been named?
When you think about your culture, or your area of the world,
   what unique gift or challenge does it offer the world church?
How can the experience of your local church enrich the understanding of the global church?

In plenary session the various caucuses reported their experience
of the consultation and how their local church might express emerging christologies and ecclesiologies. Here are some examples of a
christology and ecclesiology that emerged from the consultation.

From the African group

Christology:
Jesus as Healer (Africa is in the grips of an AIDS epidemic)
Jesus as Ancestor
Jesus as Neighbor
Jesus as Suffering Servant
Jesus as Liberator/Transformer

Ecclesiology:
The centrality of Healing Ministries
Church as Family of God
Church as Communion
Church as Servant
Church as Participation and Liberation

The Africans noted: (1) the ascending order from known to un-
known, (2) the centrality of narrative, (3) the active participation
of the entire people.

From the Australia/Asia group. They highlighted the mission of
Jesus as "where two or three are gathered . . . ," calling for open,
ecumenical, inclusive SCCs as new ways of being church. The SCCs

are silently struggling to continue the mission of Jesus. Life in the SCC points to greatly needed new structure.

From the Latin American group. The methodology of see, judge, and act is foundational to the SCCs:

(1) Begin with the real situation
(2) Illuminate it with the experience of Jesus
(3) Move to a community action—the project of Jesus
(4) Evaluate the process
(5) Celebrate

North America (a summary of the four groups). Jesus is the sacrament of God and church is the sacrament of Christ. A cohesive christology and ecclesiology are necessary.

A christology from below calls for:

Inclusiveness: multiracial communities (Jesus welcomed all at the table)
A new vision of power: power needs to function from bottom up; no downward structures
Genuine hope: God's reign is now initiating eschatology

Ecclesiology demands:

Deepening social analysis
Greater dialogue
Narrative histories of the SCCs
That the SCCs be a model for the larger church
That the SCCs facilitate conversion from primacy of control to primacy of love

Experience is crucial for SCCs producing an enfleshed christology/ecclesiology, a model of compassion. Most vexing is the place of eucharistic celebration in the small communities. Jesus in breaking bread revealed himself as a companion, a compassionate one transforming society.

While the basic movements of the method of indwelling, inquisitiveness, imagining, and inscription were evident in various activities of day three, the order was less distinct. Clearly more attention was given to imagining, as participants were asked to relate what was happening in the consultation to their particular situations.

Day Four: Emerging Theologies

The fourth day of the Consultation was devoted to inscription. In plenary session the writing team (which had spent the previous afternoon and evening at their task) presented a first draft statement attempting to capture the consultation's emerging sense of christology and ecclesiology. A spirited session on the editorial frame of the statement and the political steps to be taken provided a focus on how the reflections of the consultation might emerge to be shared with and impact the larger church.

The following editorial organization was suggested:

(1) An introduction naming the purpose and who gathered
(2) A reflection on the methodology of the consultation
(3) What practically is happening that is christological and ecclesiological in Latin America, Asia, Africa, and the U.S.? What effects are being felt in the local church, in the wider society?
(4) What christology is emerging?
(5) What ecclesiology is emerging?
(6) Conclusion: the hoped for impact of this consultation.

The methodology of the "dance" of indwelling, inquisitiveness, imagining and inscription wove through the social gatherings and bountiful dinners, coffee and tea breaks, informal meeting and sharing, an added presentation on contemporary sociological research on small communities in the U.S., various times of prayer and eucharistic liturgy (lead by various local churches), and planned and unplanned fun and relaxation.

Summary

A segment of the people of God as the *sensus fidelium*—bishops, theologians, faith community organizers, and small community members from around the world, all equals in voicing experience—gathered in a participative method to effect a new reflection of Christ and the church in a dynamic interaction between scholarly and pastoral leadership.

Participants began with an openness to each other by way of common texts—the elaborations of the theologians. They dwelt with these texts and probed them in terms of their experience in community: the themes, the challenges, the connections, and the questions that resonated with their experiences. As one community, one 'sense of the faithful,' they drew—from their collective imaginations, Scripture, church tradition, and life experiences—the images that spoke to the challenge the SCCs hold for the future understanding of Christ and the church.

In regional groupings they addressed critical issues their local churches are facing as they move into the future: the unique gift or challenge offered from their culture to the world church and how the experience of their local church enriches the understanding of the global church.

They produced a corporate articulation of what is happening practically that is christological and ecclesiological in Latin America, Asia, Africa, and North America; what effects are being felt in the local church, in the wider society; what christology is emerging; what ecclesiology is emerging and the hoped for impact of this consultation.

This consultation was a *particular* exercise of contextual theological method. In discussion at the conclusion of the consultation, participants reflected on how authentic a model of contextual theology had taken place. Some, for example, were concerned that the consultation began with the texts of theologians rather than with the voiced experiences of all present. Some expressed concern about the action to follow the consultation.

This exercise in theological method verified that each culture will exercise contextual theology in its characteristic way. The planners of this event were North Americans, heavily influenced by classical academic theology. In the North American culture contextual theology retains a great deference for academic theology, but its spirit of democracy expects its academics, its bishops, its pastoral leaders, and its people to dialogue. The method of this consultation brought these several perspectives together in communion with each other. Contextual theology in this culture is recovering a great respect for the imagination. Furthermore, North American culture is a ground of many cultures. It is learning to value and effect multicultural interactions. The context of North America is one of abundant monetary resources and these resources provided forty-five participants from eleven countries on five continents a home at Notre Dame for a week and made connections for future interactions around the globe.

The remainder of this chapter takes this experience of contextual theology into dialogue with the history of contextual theology and present-day reflections on its integration into the theological academy.

Reflections on Method in Theology

Contextual Theology—A Brief History[7]

The unfathomable destruction of human life and spirit in the two great wars of this century had the sobering effect of focusing theologians on the problems of present-day societies rather than on speculation detached from present lived experience. After the mid-point in this century, theologians, particularly in Europe, began to talk of a theology of "present realities" or contextual theology.[8] Contextual theology represents an epistemological breakthrough in doing theology. In contrast to classical theology's two norms: Scripture and tradition, contextual theology consciously recovers *experience* as a third norm. Experience becomes the point of departure and the point of return for contextual theology. Contextual theology, then, points to a renewed touchstone as an initial canon for doing its work.[9]

Latin America has been the most celebrated locale for the breakthrough in contextual theology. In 1961 Monsignor Luigi Ligutti, the Vatican's observer at the Food and Agriculture Organization of the United Nations (FAO), commissioned François Houtart, a Belgian priest teaching at the Catholic University of Louvain (who had been trained in the sociology of religion at the University of Chicago) to conduct a study of the condition of church and society in each country of Latin America.[10] Several of Houtart's Latin American students joined him in this work, and in an amazingly short period, they established centers of investigation in various cities in Latin America. Today these continue as major loci of research, training, and theologizing.

In 1963, at the request of the Consejo Episcopal Latino-Americano (CELAM, the Latin-American Episcopal Conference) Houtart summarized his investigations and translated them into English and French for distribution to the bishops attending Vatican II. CELAM appointed Houtart its council *peritus*. He made a significant contribution in providing sociological and economic descriptions of the Latin American countries.

Houtart's work influenced one of the major documents emerging from Vatican II, *Gaudium et Spes*, which altered the church's theological method.[11] Traditionally, the church had theologized deductively—that is, beginning with rational principles or articles of faith and then applying these to present situations. In contrast, *Gaudium et Spes* used an inductive method, starting with "the signs of the times" or the "here and now" of experience and then engaging theological principles in a synthesis of tradition and present fact before acting. From this base of present experience, the council exercised a new mode of theology.

From the late 1950s until the late 1960s Houtart and the University of Louvain were also affecting the church in Latin America in another way. Because Europe was viewed as the center of culture, the tradition in Latin American countries was to send rising intellectuals—artists, architects, philosophers, and theologians—there for training. Thus, generations of young theologians went to the great European theological schools to study the classic texts in order that they might raise the level of Latin American theology to the standards of Europe.

A shift in theological approach was taking place in several great European schools during the 50s and 60s, however. Specifically, at Louvain during those years was a critical mass of theology students from Latin America: Gustavo Gutiérrez, Otto Maduro, Enrique Dussel, Camilo Torres, Clodovis Boff, and others. Houtart, as a sociologist of religion, had been appointed to the theological faculty to employ critical sociology as a theological method.[12] Rather than being given the huge tomes of the classical theologians as their starting point in theological reflection, these students were invited to "look in the mirror"—that is, to begin with themselves as the place to find the action of God.

This was difficult at first, since the students had learned to think of the Latin American situation as an embarrassment when compared with the cultures of Europe. Yet as they came to envision their situation as an experience of the presence of God, these students began to find God revealed in the very conditions of oppression so characteristic of their world. They began to accept the identity of a poor suffering people as their own identity. Thus their theology became characterized as a theology of liberation, since the gospel of Christ in the Latin American reality of the masses of the people was the good news that salvation meant freedom from centuries of oppression.

It is important to recognize also the contributions of young university men and women in Latin America as part of the Young Christian Students (YCS) movement of the 1950s. Its method of see, judge, and act had evolved into a "Christian left" movement, with analysis of and action on the structures of society.[13] Thus, the ground had been prepared for the reform of church and society. When the young clerics came back from Europe, there was a validation of this vision of theology because of YCS.

To claim that the theology of liberation had its origin in Europe would be improper; yet Louvain and the other centers there did foster a "theology of temporal realities."[14] It was a generic theological methodology to be specified in different contexts. In Latin America this approach became known as "Liberation Theology." In the second and third major gatherings of Latin American bishops and theologians (CELAM) at Medellín, Columbia (1968), and at

Puebla, Mexico (1979), Latin Americans both interpreted and contextualized the work of the Second Vatican Council.

At Medellín, "people of God," the image of church that guided
Vatican II, was translated in light of the great need for community amid the fragmentation and anonymity of modern urban life.
In the ten years between Medellín and Puebla, "the Latin American
Church forged its own distinctive profile, matured in personality,
and shaped its own contribution to both the local church and the
universal world Church." It did this by incorporating the Christian
base communities as *the* instrumentality for transformation of the
church and society, the concrete expression of "the people of God."
In this way Latin Americans contextualized Vatican II.[15]

Particularly in Brazil, the hierarchy recognized these SCCs as the
new form of church the institutional church needed to develop. The
SCCs became part of the pastoral plan of the church in Brazil, part
of its attempt locally to carry out the reforms of Vatican II as articulated at Medellín and Puebla.[16]

Through the base community church, the people of Latin America were, for the first time, seeing a union between their religion and
their church. They said, "We are the church," rather than "We are
in the church," a movement from being objects to being subjects.
The church was no longer distant from the people but had become
intimate with their experience. Latin Americans viewed their experience (oppression) in religious terms. The rich-poor structure of
their society was challenged by equality in the reign of God. Religious and political identities came into critical dialogue. The dual-
isms between religion and church, faith and life, ceased to exist.
Consequently, the church in Latin America became a most feared
presence and the Bible was considered a subversive document.[17]

The Primacy of Community for Contextual Theology

In our day, Christian religious scholars have looked to Latin
America as the most significant locus for change in church. Latin
American liberation theologians have been attempting since the late
1950s to work alongside the people, especially the poor, to change
their social realities of political, economic, and social violence and
oppression. Local people in many Latin American countries have

been banding together, managing their fear, and changing their environment through the instrumentality of Christian base communities.[18] They have been creating "church" in new ways, transforming a major institution in their world, the Catholic Church, by balancing hierarchy and community. In these basic communities, they have become educated, both secularly and religiously, and have thereby been empowered to make a certain degree, sometimes significant, of transformative social change.[19]

Leonardo Boff calls this development "ecclesiogenesis." He notes: "The history of the church is not merely the history of the actualization of ancient forms or of a return to the pristine experiences of the historical past. The history of the church is a genuine history: the creation of never before experienced novelty."[20] Boff holds a developmental view of history in which the church as community, like all other forms of life, is continually emerging.

Boff describes this emergence of church through the story of Latin America's Christian base communities, where the people build community upon intimate participation in living the essence of the Christian message. He asserts that modern society has violated the principles needed for the development of community, resulting in atomization and anonymity. Persons have become lost in the mechanisms of macro-organization. Community life has undergone significant redevelopment in Latin America in the past thirty years. Rapid changes have produced major dislocations, especially in the transfer of capital and other resources from its underdeveloped countries. In grass-roots communities relationships are direct; there is reciprocity, a deep communion, mutual assistance, commonality of ideals, equality among members. There is an absence of alienating structures, rigid rules, and prescribed relationships.[21]

Boff analyzes the relationship between the Christian base community and the institutional church as requiring a mixture of the communitarian and the societal. He contends the Christian base communities are communities *within* the church society. The relationship of community and society is beyond Tönnies's dichotomy of *Gemeinschaft* and *Gesellschaft*. Community is "society's utopia."[22] Tension between the organizational/impersonal and the intimate/personal is inevitable. Community is a spirit to be created, not an institutional state to be achieved—an inspiration to bend one's constant efforts toward overcoming barriers between persons and to generate a relationship of solidarity and reciprocity. The actualization of the communal spirit comes more easily in small groups. Any large organization can be renewed *by* a community, but it cannot be transformed into a community. Christianity, Boff holds, is essentially oriented to the creation, within societal structures, of the communitarian spirit. The problem is not the counterpoint of institution and community. This tension is forever. The problem is to have the two respect each other in their order of precedence. Community has primacy; institution exists to serve community; community requires adequate institutional expression.[23]

The Reconstruction of Academic Theology

David Tracy, concerned because theology tends not to address the religious in the contemporary human struggle, recasts the categories of theology to activate a "critical correlation between an interpretation of the Christian fact and the contemporary situation," i.e., between theological abstraction and life.[24]

Tracy's first work phenomenologically establishes that fundamental theology's task is to show *that* human experience is, at its heart, religious.[25] His second work describes constructive or systematic theology as an attempt to express this human religious experience in terms of the classic Christian texts or traditions.[26] Systematic theology's mode, then, is that of literary analysis. Thus, Tracy calls for an "analogical imagination." He proposed a third book to develop the position that the work of practical theology is to construct a model or vision of human transformation—what people "live" when they operate from the Christian tradition.[27] This *vision* is a synthesis of fundamental theology's *assertion* of human experience's religious nature (thesis) and systematic theology's *expression* of this experience in Christian terms [religious analogy] (antithesis). A synthesis according to Tracy's philosopher, Hegel, "preserves, uplifts, and transforms" the thesis and antithesis all simultaneously. Thus, Tracy's construction of the relationship of ways of thinking theologically about religious experience is threefold: *intuitive*—common to human experience, *narrative*—as analogy in religious texts, and thirdly, *expressive*—as vision in action. For Tracy there can be no one way or handmaid relationship among the categories of theology nor the categories of theologians. The pastoral agent—the "practical theologian"—for Tracy is the one who calls forth the living vision of human transformation that comes by *living* ethically in the world. Her or his activity participates in the theological task by its struggle to formulate the *telos* or vision of the human religious experience, what Tracy calls the ethical ideal.

A problem with classical theological epistemology is that the intellectuals' sources are not the primary sources. The primary source is experience. This is the model of the Bible, a record of primary sources. Theology or religious theory is secondary reflections on these primary sources. We have confused secondary sources for primary sources.

Knowing Is in Action

In the model of technical rationality, the world of knowledge is built upon a vision of control and a desire for efficiency in action. Now, however, scholars are more aware of the importance and value of complexity, uncertainty, instability, uniqueness, and value conflicts. These conditions that exist in the pastoral field are not to be abstracted and dealt within the theological "ivy tower," but are the loci of knowing in their own contexts. What is central to the pastoral agent is not theory of how to solve a problem and its principles, but reflective action.

The old epistemology of action was shaped by a concern with problem solving; the new epistemology of "reflective action" is not. It is concerned with "problem setting." Where "technical rationality" cannot tolerate uncertainty, reflective action is secure in dealing with uncertainty; where technical rationality only operates scientifically, reflective action operates artistically; and where technical rationality is restricted to a single discipline, reflective action chooses from among competing professional paradigms.

The pastoral agent, then, is the theological actor who has the power to decide on her or his feet. Only on the hard high ground can one follow research-based theory and technique; in the swamps it is too messy. Yet it is in the swamps where the problems of greatest human need exist. It is precisely this concern about religion's relevance to human problems that has caused Tracy to revise theology.

Theological education needs to see theological research not just as a product, but as a process—something in which to engage. The operative epistemology here is that *knowing is in action.* Action needs to be seen as embodying thinking. Ordinarily, there are not rules and plans in mind before acting; knowing happens in action.

In *A Fundamental Practical Theology*, Don Browning elaborated a reframing of theological education that lives out the theological *habitus* as a "rhythm of theologizing."[28] This rhythm flows from action to theory and back to action through four movements: *describing* the community's action, *analyzing* this action historically, *systematically relating* life themes in the action to the religious tradition, and *establishing the norms and strategies* of pastoral response to the action.

Thus Browning sees "Practical Theology" (or contextual theology) not as a discipline but as an overview of theology itself, the indication that theology arises out of the lived experience of the community. Like a font of water coming from the ground, ever new and alive, the actions of the community are the source of its theology.

Conclusion

Latin America has been the most celebrated exercise of contextual theology and the Latin Americans were a significant voice in this consultation, "older brothers and sisters" reminding the consultants of the starting place of contextual theology and its end point—the same locus, the experience of God's people. Pastoral activity that transforms society has also been the object of contextual theology and is the concern of this consultation's reflection, not merely writing a book. The knowledge expressed is knowing that comes from and ends in action.

The voice of the members of church as small community was engaged in this consultation by the voice of both academics and pastoral leaders to become one voice, a true theological *habitus* in which there was a flow from action (experience) to theory, to policy and strategy, and back to experience (action). This special relationship of the people, their pastoral shepherds, theologians, and pastoral agents was an incarnation of contextual theology, truly a consultation of the faithful.

Notes

1. B. J. Fleischer, "A Theological Method for Adult Education Rooted in the Works of Tracy and Lonergan," paper given at the Association for Researchers and Professors in Religious Education, New Orleans, November 1996, p. 1.

2. S. B. Bevans, *Models of Contextual Theology* (Maryknoll, N.Y.: Orbis Books, 1994).

3. B. J. Lee, S.M. "Praxic Theology: A Talking Paper" delivered at the AAR/SBL session on Practical Theology, November, New Orleans, 1996, p. 1.

4. This grass-roots activity (participatory theological research) sees theology as *participative* endeavor: where the people are seen as producers (subjects) of theological knowledge, not merely its objects. The professional leader researches *with*, not *for* the people. Accountability lies with the people, in contrast to classical research based upon the "capitalist" division of labor where some think, others work.

Theological research from this popular (base) perspective means doing theological research for the purpose of action on behalf of the needs of the people. That is, a moral commitment is necessary for the understanding of truth. The topics come from the people. Popular (*desde abajo*) theological research challenges the belief that the disenfranchised have no voice and are incompetent. It does not just make "official knowledge" available for the people, it affirms popular knowledge.

5. J. Sobrino, *The True Church and the Poor* (Maryknoll, N.Y.: Orbis Books, 1984), p. 8.

6. Anne Reisner of the Maryknoll Center for Mission Research, who served as facilitator of the consultation, provided this framework.

7. Some of the historical reflections in this section are adapted from Robert T. O'Gorman, "Latin American Theology and Education" in *Theological Approaches to Christian Education*, edited by Jack L. Seymour and Donald E. Miller (Nashville: Abingdon Press, 1990). Copyright © Abingdon, used by permission.

8. F. Houtart, "La Contribution de L'Universite Catholique de Louvain au Developpement de la Sociologie de la Religion en Amerique Latine." April 4, 1985. A mimeograph of Centre de Recherches Socio-Religieuses, Section: Religion et Developpement, Universite Catholique de Louvain, 1348—Ottignies—Louvain-la-Neuve, Belgium.

9. Sobrino, *The True Church and the Poor.*

10. Personal interview with François Houtart, October 1986.

11. In the English-speaking world, this document was called *The Church in the Modern World;* in the Spanish-speaking world, *The Church in the World Today,* or more literally, *The Church in the Here and Now.* On the influence of Latin American bishops on *Gaudium et Spes,* see Marcos McGrath, "The Impact of *Gaudium et Spes," The Church and Culture since Vatican II,* ed. Joseph Gremillion (Notre Dame, Ind.: University of Notre Dame Press, 1985). At the council, Latin American bishops chose identification with the poor, rather than accommodation with modernity chosen by the English speakers.

12. Interview with Houtart, 1986.

13. The movement known as Catholic Action encouraged students only to see, judge, and act as an extension of the hierarchy. The development of a "Christian left" allowed them to act with their own sense of individuality yet retain their Catholic identity; see Edward L. Cleary, O.P., *Crisis and Change* (Maryknoll, N.Y.: Orbis Books, 1985) and Daniel S. Schipani, *Religious Education Encounters Liberation Theology* (Birmingham, Ala.: Religious Education Press, 1988).

14. François Houtart, 1985.

15. M. de C. Azevedo, S.J., *Basic Ecclesial Communities in Brazil* (Washington, D.C.: Georgetown University Press, 1987), p. 85.

16. Ibid.

17. R. Shaull, *Heralds of a New Reformation* (Maryknoll, N.Y.: Orbis Press, 1984).

18. Azevedo (1987).

19. P. Freire, *Pedagogy of the Oppressed* (New York: Herder and Herder, 1970).

20. L. Boff, *Ecclesiogenesis: The Base Communities Reinvent the Church* (Maryknoll, N.Y.: Orbis Books, 1986), p. 2.

21. This message entails the universal parenthood of God, communion with all beings, celebration of the presence of Jesus Christ resurrected in Eucharist, and the building up of the kingdom as the liberation of the whole human being and all human beings.

22. Boff, 1986, p. 2.

23. The institutional church lives alongside the other great social and cultural institutions, enjoying social power and serving as an interlocutor with the powers of society. The communitarian church lives in the network of base communities, living the horizontal relationships of co-responsibility and communion on the margins of power and influence over society. Church as institution needs the church as community to hold on to the spirit of Jesus as it moves in the world of other institutions. The church as communities needs the church as institution for continuity, for their Catholic identity, and for their oneness with one another. It is in the convergence and differentiation (dialectical interaction) between these two dimensions that the Church as a whole exists and develops (Boff, 1986).

24. D. S. Browning, quoting Tracy in *Practical Theology: The Emerging Field in Theology, Church, and World* (San Francisco: Harper and Row, 1983), p. 61.

25. D. Tracy, *Blessed Rage for Order: The New Pluralism in Theology* (New York: Seabury, 1975).

26. D. Tracy, *The Analogical Imagination: Christian Theology and the Culture of Pluralism* (New York: Crossroad Books, 1981).

27. D. Tracy, *Plurality and Ambiguity: Hermeneutics, Religion, Hope* (San Francisco: Harper and Row, 1987).

28. Don S. Browning, *A Fundamental Practical Theology: Descriptive and Strategic Proposals* (Minneapolis: Augsburg Fortress, 1991).

CHRISTOLOGIES EMERGING FROM THE SMALL CHRISTIAN COMMUNITIES

Monika K. Hellwig

The Christology taught and discussed at major theological schools around the world has been challenged and influenced substantially in the last several decades by voices coming from small grass-roots communities. This has usually been mediated by networks of theologically sophisticated facilitators of such communities, usually among the poor and oppressed. For some time it has been the concern of these facilitators to present the Gospels without commentary and to listen receptively to the reflections that are voiced in the Christian base communities. The intent has been to acknowledge the *sensus fidelium* as truly operating in our own time, that is to say to acknowledge that the community living by the Spirit is guided in its understanding and discernment by the Spirit and is therefore an authentic source of Christian teaching.

Two theoretical grounds have been invoked to justify the process of drawing on the testimony of the Christian base communities as a source for theology. The first ground is the general one of the primacy of *praxis*. This is the understanding that any theory, such as theology, does not drop from heaven or arise from pure thought without a context in practical experience; practical engagement with reality precedes reflection upon it and formulation of an understanding. But if this is so, then the process does not stop at some point to be crystallized in a timeless, universally valid formula of words. Experience continues and reflection continues in successive times, cultures, circumstances. Formulae taken over from the past must be related to their own context to be understood and cannot substitute for the reflection of the present upon the present experience of new peoples in new cultures and circumstances.

Added to this general ground for a theology arising from grass-roots reflection on grass-roots experience is another foundational principle. It has been named the hermeneutic privilege of the poor and has provided a special reason for listening attentively to the many Christian base communities which belong to the poor countries, to oppressed or despised populations, to the poor or outcast of rich countries. The thesis is that Jesus lived among poor, colonized, subjugated, and oppressed people and, among them, tended to turn particularly to those least favored in every way. His actions and words, therefore, can be best understood by those who labor under similar disadvantages. Moreover, the preaching and presence of Jesus were a promise of redemption, of salvation, and would therefore be best understood by those who could not but be keenly and immediately aware of their unfreedom and misery, their need to be set free and saved.

The impact on contemporary Christology, therefore, has been not only from the reflection of grass-roots Christian communities in general, but in a special way from that of such groups among poor and oppressed peoples. There is a bold freshness in what emerges, because poor people are usually very little educated and therefore also less indoctrinated on theological topics. Given a sense of their own personhood and proper encouragement, they can respond creatively out of their own experience because they cannot fall back on pat answers out of books that are familiar but not always understood. Indeed, it is the endeavor of prayerful small Christian communities among the privileged and educated to come to this happy condition of truly reflecting on Scripture in the light of one's own experience and not with pat answers alien to that experience.

Increasingly in the twentieth century, and especially as the conclusions of the Second Vatican Council came to be more widely understood and assimilated, Christian base communities have been confronting the text of Scripture directly, not through doctrinal mediation, and have focused more usually on shared reading and meditation on the Gospels. Out of this has come a mode of Christology which is ascending, contextualized, practical, and political. Each of these aspects needs to be explained further.

"Ascending Christology" is a term that was brought into wide circulation by Karl Rahner, but what has emerged from the grass-roots reflection has gone far beyond Rahner. In his case, the term "ascending Christology" simply meant that instead of beginning with an attempt to understand (or even define) what is meant by the divinity claim for Christ, one should begin with a careful consideration of what it means to be human and should apply to an understanding of Jesus all the essential aspects of being human before reflecting on what it means to say that Jesus is divine. This was a great breakthrough in theology earlier in the twentieth century. However, it tended to be very abstract and to think about being human quite without considering context or relationships with other people or bodily needs or gender, race, history, political setting and so forth. It was an abstract way of thinking about humanness, such as a professor might indulge in the pleasant quiet of his study without having to worry about where the dinner was coming from or remembering that he was once an infant with no critical ability at all but an urgent need to have his diapers changed.

What the voices of the Christian base communities have added to this is a mighty dose of reality. Meditating together on the Jesus of the Gospels, they have brought their varied experience to bear upon the various stories of what Jesus did and said and what happened to him. They have imagined the scenes from their own experience of being human, almost always in situations far less sheltered and privileged than those of most theologians of modern times. These groups have consisted of people who did not have the same need for instant abstraction but tended to enter into scenes and conversations of the Gospels by bridges of empathy and analogy out of their own concrete experience. When we read accounts like *Gospel in Solentiname* we see people using analogy to move from the concrete to the concrete. We see people who do not forget that Jesus and his friends ate, drank, slept, laughed, and sneezed and found ways of coping with difficult situations by trial and error. Like Jesus and his friends, many of the Christian base communities are close to the soil, knowing the smell of sweat, the feel of aching muscles, the reality of human interdependence.

However, it is not only in this broadly analogous way that the Jesus of the small Christian communities tends to be more solid, more truly human in bodiliness and historicity. Out of the continuing concern with discipleship, many groups have found that in trying to understand what the teachings of Jesus meant for them they had a need to understand them first of all in his own context. There was, of course, already a keen scholarly interest in biblical and ecumenical circles to understand Jesus as a Jew among Jews, using the language and customs and worship of his people and addressing himself to his fellow Jews. But the further thrust from the grassroots groups among the poor and among activists was to ask what the teachings of Jesus mean for the political and economic problems of our own societies today. These questions certainly found substantial support and reinforcement in the documents of Vatican II, more particularly in *Gaudium et Spes*. Thus the reflections and questions that came from such groups demanded first of those theologians who were facilitators among them, and then gradually of the theologians in the theological schools, a now kind of quest of the historical Jesus—a quest to understand better his relationship, passive and active, with the economic and political challenges of his time. J. B. Metz, for instance, who more than any of his colleagues had interested himself in the political dimensions of Christian theology, admits that this took on a completely different, more concrete and particular, meaning for him in consequence of his contacts with the liberation theologians of Latin America, reflecting to him the questions of discipleship that arose from the Christian base communities of that continent.

The underlying difference in the Christology arising out of the small Christian communities from the conventional Christology of the schools surely lies in the motivation and the starting point. Since mediaeval times in the Western churches, theology has largely been seen as a quite separate enterprise from spirituality. One studies theology formally in order to qualify as one who knows, who is an expert, who can play the intellectual games by the proper rules and perhaps as one who can add to the scholarship, certainly as one who knows and can judge orthodoxy. In many cases orthodoxy is valued above intelligibility. The Christology that arises out of grass-roots small communities is practical in its origin, its intention, its methods, and its goals. These groups reflect on the Gospels, the sources at hand, to learn how to live and act and what they might hope for. From the outset they take a practical approach. It ordinarily does not occur to them to discuss "who" Jesus is, or "what his nature is"; they look at what Jesus does, and listen to what he says, empathize with those he heals or encourages or scolds. They try to understand what his message is, what wisdom he teaches, what salvation he envisages. Their interest is operational and not ontological.

Related to this is the fact that in many instances both hierarchic Church and secular state have been appalled and antagonized by the exposure of the intrinsically and inevitably political character of the gospel of Jesus when it is consistently lived out. The discipleship quest of Christian base communities has unmasked the Constantinian Christ, the guarantor of existing power structures, as an impostor. A consistent discipleship quest unfolds the vision of Jesus in quest of the Reign of God, a keenly critical, countercultural figure, calling for the conversion of persons and also of the structures in which their relationships and behavior are expressed. Any group meditation on Jesus in the Gospels which is undertaken with a view to more faithful discipleship in our day, with our knowledge of social, economic, and political dynamics in the world, seems to come very quickly to the Cross as the sign of contradiction. Such group meditation comes very quickly to the realization that the symbolism of the Cross has been misused when it has been proposed as a reason to accept the injustice and suffering in the world as God's will, a reason to interpret God as a figure of vengeance who must be appeased by the suffering of the innocent while the guilty continue to oppress in order to feed their greed for wealth and power. The Cross becomes rather the sign of the one who will risk and suffer all in order to challenge all that is amiss in the uses of power, spiritual and temporal—to challenge it by setting out the vision of the Reign of God in human society in all its aspects.

To the extent that small Christian communities are either among the poor and oppressed or move into solidarity with the poor and oppressed, certain features emerge in the Christology that is either made explicit or is adumbrated. The first of these is the primacy of soteriology in the understanding of Christ. The soteriology is not built on a prior ontological claim about the simultaneous divinity and humanity of Jesus. It is rather that the picture of Jesus and of the risen Christ that is constructed emerges out of the ongoing concern to participate actively in his saving action in the world, seen as penetrating all this-worldly matters.

A second clear feature that emerges is the centrality of compassion in what Jesus is seen to do and what discipleship is understood to mean. And along with this central impulse of compassion goes a certain earthiness in the understanding of what Jesus meant by the Reign of God and what that should mean in the life and activity of the Christian today. There is a reassertion of human freedom and creativity in the redemption. Just as the focus tends to be on the humanity of Jesus as both imitable and significant, so the model for the disciple is not one of total passivity but of creativity empowered by grace. Jesus who gives his disciples the gift of the Holy Spirit models empowerment to act redemptively in human creativity. God does not act alongside of the human but precisely in Jesus and in his graced, en-Spirited followers.

If the above reading of the impact of the Christian base communities on Christology is correct, it should come as no surprise that this tremendous reawakening of Spirit in grass-roots communities in the Church is arousing fear, suspicion, and even outright hostility among good people in the Church. There is in the first place the underlying assumption of the primacy of *praxis* in relation to theory. Since the fourth century we have tended to place orthodoxy above orthopraxis and have tended to define orthodoxy in terms of specific verbal definitions, faith in terms of believing, and obedience to God as practically coincident with obedience to Church authority and teaching. The notion that the practice of discipleship is a quest in which individuals and communities of disciples constantly bring questions from their own engagement with reality into confrontation with the Jesus of the Gospels—this notion is in head-on conflict with the picture of the Constantinian Emperor Christ authorizing all present uses of established temporal and spiritual power. What emerges is a revolutionary rather than a validating Christ. If the reading of the Gospels is consistent, this Christ will be a gentle, nonviolent but prophetically critical revolutionary figure, but it is inevitable that those whose securities and certainties are questioned will perceive violence and coming chaos, and they will find it safer to crucify the challengers.

From a slightly different angle there is another kind of challenge in the idea of the hermeneutic privilege of the poor. For a long time now we have not even granted the hermeneutic privilege of the heroically committed, and there has boon a tendency in the hierarchic authority to question the hermeneutic privilege of the scholar and the better informed, reducing all to the exclusive hermeneutic privilege of the hierarchic magisterium. The question of who may interpret and with what degree of authority this may be done is one that will not be easily resolved into a general consensus in the Church. And this relates immediately to the issues in ecclesiology, in our understanding of the Church and its life and activity, which will be the concerns of the second paper and the second day's discussion. These questions about the Church are intimately and inevitably linked to the way we understand what Jesus was about and what is therefore the task of the followers of Jesus throughout history into our own time and beyond. These questions are also intimately related, therefore, to what we understand to be the goal or end result of the redemption, the content of hope to which Jesus pointed the way.

Many of the conflicts which have arisen in the Church in our time have come about because Vatican II awoke a new understanding of the role of the laity as People of God and of the importance of direct access to the Scriptures for all the People of God. There is no doubt that communal reflection on Scripture has been at the heart of the small Christian communities of all kinds which have formed in many parts of the world, in many different cultures and economic and social conditions. This attraction to Scripture has focused on the Gospels and the understanding of what Jesus was about and what he hoped his followers would do to carry on his mission. That question is being pursued with great passion by many people who are seeing the faith they formerly took for granted in a new light and who are discovering a dynamism in it which challenges static formulae and static structures which may have outlasted their intelligibility and their aptness for the quest. This inevitably causes tension, because all do not grow at the same speed or in the same direction and some are afraid of growth, seeing it as a denial of the changelessness of God's dispensation.

It seems to be a time for great patience but not the patience of inactivity—rather the patience of respectful dialogue in a context of prayerfulness and listening for the voice of the Spirit in the voice of the other, while not denying it within one's own experience and prayerful discernment. It is clear that, followed consistently, a Christology drawn from ongoing discipleship will be led in the truth by the Spirit of Jesus, and often that is more clearly discerned by placing it in the context of the long history of the church which has brought us to our present understanding and our present questions about Jesus and his project.

RESPONSE

Aylward E. M. Shorter, M.Afr.

Dr. Hellwig has given a clear exposition of the general grounds for a theology arising from the small Christian communities: the primacy of praxis and the need for continuous reflection on experience. She has also mentioned the foundational principle of the hermeneutical privilege of the poor. Most of her paper, however, is devoted to the notion and implications of an ascending christology, which she takes to be characteristic of the theological reflection of the small Christian communities.

I am in broad agreement with her, and all I would like to do in this response is to illustrate her argument with reference to the small Christian communities (SCCs) of Eastern Africa and especially to my own experience of working with these communities in urban Nairobi. This will also allow me to introduce some nuances into Dr. Hellwig's thesis.

De facto the SCCs of Eastern Africa are a grass-roots phenomenon that has arisen among the poor in a number of countries in the region; therefore the principles of a preferential option for the poor and the hermeneutical privilege of the poor are applicable. However, from their inception, the *rationale* of these small Christian communities was not poverty as such, but the fact that they represent a given life-context within which Christians are called to live their faith. They represent, therefore, Dr. Hellwig's theoretical grounds: of practical engagement with reality and the relationship of theology to a particular context—in other words, the primacy of praxis.

Founded, as it is, on a praxis, the theological reflection of these small Christian communities employs the first-order language of faith, rather than the second-order language of systematic theology and metaphysics (to apply a distinction drawn by J. H. Newman). This reflection, however, is nonetheless genuine theology—"faith seeking understanding." It also constitutes an original reinterpretation of both gospel and local culture. I have said many times (because I believe it to be profoundly true) that small Christian com-

munities in Africa are the principal agents and guarantors of inculturation, which is the encounter of the Christian faith-tradition
with the living traditions of Africa.

This encounter takes place through the central activity of the
small Christian communities, which is the communal reflection on
Scripture. This, as Dr. Hellwig rightly points out, is at the heart of
SCCs. There are many types of such communities. It has even been
said that each small Christian community differs in kind from all
the others. However, it is safe to say that the activity of biblical
reflection unites most, if not all of them. It is true, as Dr. Hellwig
says, that in the small Christian communities people move from the
concrete to the concrete and that they imagine the biblical scenes
from their own experience of being human. This is demonstrated in
the biblical dramatizations and Bible-inspired morality plays which
the SCCs contribute to the liturgical celebrations in the urban slum
parish with which I am associated for my part-time ministry.

It is also true that the humanity of Jesus is the focus of theological reflection in the SCCs. One form which this takes is in the image
of the Church as the family of God. This was an important theme
of the 1994 African Synod, but it echoes an emphasis already to be
found, both in the life of the SCCs and in the writings of African
theologians. The family is also central to the understanding, organization, and worship of traditional ethnic religion in Africa. SCCs
feel themselves to be part of the family of Jesus. He is the "elder
brother." He is also the divine "ancestor," according to a mentality
which views ancestors as being integral to the living family community and which also regards God as the ultimate ancestor and source
of all being.

In rural areas, where village settlements, and the SCCs that are
identified with them, frequently follow family and kinship patterns,
there are obvious problems in implementing the concept of a family
of God which transcends the natural human family. In urban areas
SCCs stand a better chance of serving as a surrogate family, because—sadly—family institutions and values are at a discount in the
urban context. The image of the spiritual family of Jesus, however,
strongly appeals to SCCs in Africa ("Anyone who does the will of

my Father in heaven is my brother, my sister, and my mother" (Mt. 12:50).

Another aspect of the humanity of Jesus celebrated by the SCCs in Africa concerns his compassion (mentioned by Dr. Hellwig) and his activity as a healer. Jesus the "diviner healer" is a popular image, and it relates to ordinary people's concern with sickness and health and to the activities of the SCCs in caring for, and praying with, the sick.

Although this is less true in the urban context, SCCs in Africa tend to have a geographical dimension and to identify with a particular neighborhood. Neighborhood is an important experience of traditional African village society. There are neighborhood celebrations and neighborhood courts to resolve disputes. African oral tradition abounds in references to the relationship of neighbors. Consequently, the idea of Jesus as neighbor appeals very strongly to the SCCs. "As long as you did it to one of these, you did it to me" (Matt. 25:40). In the service of one another, members of the SCCs encounter Jesus as neighbor.

Dr. Hellwig is correct in her perception that SCCs, in their meditation on the person of Jesus, come very quickly to the Cross as sign of contradiction. One of the major celebrations in which the SCCs are involved, in the Nairobi parish to which I go, is Good Friday. Each SCC carries its own cross to the parish church, performing the Way of the Cross en route. There are several circuits. These pass through the squatter areas, with their scenes of destitution and despair, and all converge on the church in time for the Good Friday liturgy. The crosses are set up in front of the altar. There are also banners, with messages that proclaim the faith and hope of the SCCs in facing various life problems. These banners are afterwards sewn together to make a grave-cloth which is suspended from the main crucifix during Eastertide. The veneration of the huge rough-hewn lenten cross during the Good Friday liturgy is one of the most impressive experiences in the parish. The SCCs come forward in groups of twenty to twenty-five people and remain immobile, crouched over the wood for several minutes, their foreheads touching the surface. The Good Friday liturgy thus makes an explicit link between the passion of Jesus and the "passion in the present tense" of ordinary people in the SCCs.

In spite of this, SCCs in Eastern Africa are probably less revolutionary and less political than their Latin American counterparts. Prompted by various forms of networking, such as the groups of parish animators (*wakolezaji*), the SCCs are beginning to identify justice and peace issues, which they bring to the parish justice and peace committee for subsequent action. The main focus of the SCCs in Eastern Africa, however, is pastoral rather than political. Dr. Hellwig has mentioned the clash between the hermeneutic privilege of the poor *vis-à-vis* the hermeneutic privilege of the magisterium and the issues in ecclesiology that arise from this. In Eastern Africa it is not so much a question of authoritative interpretation as of practical tension between hierarchy and communion in the life of the Church.

The SCCs in Eastern Africa are ecclesial because they are at the service of the parish pastoral team, as well as being at the service of the world, represented by their immediate neighborhood. They are not directly part of the hierarchy or territorial structure of the Church. They are "free-floating," and their membership is generally restricted to a relatively small number of core Catholics. However, they are "Church" in a more explicit sense than that in which the family is "domestic Church." They are, in fact, an extension of the pastoral team—animators of the whole parish.

Inevitably, the SCCs represent a form of collaborative ministry, in which men, women, and children all play their part. This is, in a way, prophetical, since such collaboration is not at all obvious at higher levels in the Church. Women especially are prominent in the life and ministry of the SCCs, and the youth (which constitutes nearly 80 percent of Nairobi City's population) are increasingly undertaking tasks of evangelization. As an image of the Mystical Body and of the "whole Christ," the SCCs are certainly eloquent.

Dr. Hellwig concluded her paper with remarks about the conflicts, fears, suspicion, and hostility which have been aroused in some quarters of the Church by the witness of the SCCs. No doubt this accounts for much of the reticence concerning SCCs which one finds in the official documents of the magisterium. Like Dr. Hellwig, I believe in patient dialogue, prayerful discernment, and mutual trust as the basis for ongoing discipleship and for listening to the voice of the Spirit speaking through these vibrant communities. In my own mind there is no doubt whatever that the rise of the SCCs is one of the most important things that have happened to the Church in this century.

RESPONSE

Barbara A. Howard

Dr. Monica Hellwig insightfully describes the experience of small Christian communities as that of striving to discover the experience of Jesus within Scripture and subsequently to model that experience in the events of their everyday lives. In the midst of diverse yet very real cultural, economic, and political circumstances, SCC members attempt to discern how do I love God, my neighbor, and myself in the concrete events of my life. "What did Jesus do?" becomes the operative question in formulating reflection and action.

As we share our own stories in community and compare them with the story of Jesus recounted in Scripture, we come to an understanding of a Jesus passionately involved in the lives of real people. Our relationship with Jesus is no longer mediated solely through the magisterial teaching of the hierarchical church but is born of the sorrow and joy, struggle and celebration of our lives. In small Christian community we understand that our walk is *together*, not as a small oasis of security standing against an unsympathetic world, but as a part of the body of Christ missioned to proclaim that the reign of God is among us—here and now, as well as awaiting us in its fullness at the Second Coming.

Proclaiming the reign of God necessarily means that we attempt, prayerfully and through the power of the Spirit, to do as Jesus did. As we become more adept at reflecting on our attitudes and actions vis-à-vis our understanding of the mission of Jesus, we expand these reflections to ever broader circles of human experience. By reflecting on the questions, "Who is God? Who is Neighbor? Who am I?" we enter into complex areas of human and social interaction. Basing her comments on the work of Johannes Metz, Dr. Hellwig suggests, the reflections of small Christian communities hold both potential and real danger for structures and systems that diminish rather than enhance the human dignity inherent in Jesus' proclamation of God's reign.

In Central and South America, small Christian communities understand that God's reign necessitates not only a personal moral life but also a just distribution of the world's resources within the framework of a preferential option for the poor. As Latin American communities have acted on this understanding, they have become a danger to unjust systems and have themselves become targets of further injustices perpetrated by those very systems.

More affluent, first-world SCCs are beginning to struggle with the concept of a preferential option for the poor. They are attempting to expand the call to discipleship to encompass not only personal and family morality but also to explore the much larger area of social justice and the demands that God's reign makes in the name of justice. This is a difficult move for many first-world small Christian communities whose members are constantly bombarded by the demands of individualism, consumerism, and in the United States the tradition of complete separation of church and state. But the move is a necessary one in order to bring about a more moral and just world in which Jesus' compassion, healing, and liberation can be made visible.

As SCCs read and reflect on Scripture, we take comfort in realizing the model in which we gather was the model in which Jesus gathered the first disciples. They were a small group of culturally-conditioned people who didn't always get along, who often didn't understand, who wanted to do the right thing but often got it wrong, but who spent time together trying to learn from Jesus, who came to serve and save humanity. As Jesus was patient yet challenging with his disciples, so we also learn to be patient with ourselves, with one another, and with the process of conversion that challenges us to speak and act in behalf of God's reign.

The journey of conversion which we have undertaken as members of small Christian communities is a path which many people are now traveling. We hope to walk this journey in the company of all our brothers and sisters, rich and poor, powerful and weak, lay, religious, clergy, and bishops. We understand the power of Christ's Spirit present in the stories of faith and life we share with one an-

other. We know the inherent potential which lies in a shared life
dedicated to living and acting as Jesus did. We hope in a future
where the people of God in both large and small church are not
only a voice of conscience but a body of disciples acting in solidarity
with the Jesus who proclaimed

> The Spirit of the Lord is upon me,
> because he has anointed me
> to bring glad tidings to the poor.
> He has sent me to proclaim liberty to captives
> and recovery of sight to the blind,
> to let the oppressed go free,
> and to proclaim a year acceptable to the Lord.
>
> (Luke 4: 18–19)

UNCANNY GRACE

Christian Communities and the Survival of Hope

Curt Cadorette, M.M.

There are many possible ways to begin a discussion of emerging forms of Christian community. My choice is to start with a home-spun analysis of a foundational Christian document, the Gospel of Mark. In particular, I want to focus on the fifth chapter. As is typical of Mark, highly succinct narrative is packed with theological meaning. In the fifth chapter of the Gospel, Mark tells three seemingly separate but ultimately interrelated stories that are filled with information about Jesus, God's reign, and the women and men who make up the Christian community. In rapid order the author describes three healings, the Gerasene demoniac, the raising of Jairus' daughter, and sandwiched into this second incident, the woman with a hemorrhage. A madman, a sick and impoverished woman, and a dead child seem like unlikely recipients of grace and symbols of God's reign. They are all ritually unclean and their situations appear hopelessly dire. Obviously, that is Mark's point. Three desperate people confound the somber resignation of those around them who would bind them with chains, counsel resignation, or accept prema-ture death as a given. God's grace and reign, embodied in Jesus and those he heals, are swift and unpredictable. They stretch our imagi-nations in miraculous ways.

In contemporary psychological language, the Gerasene demoniac is psychotic. His self-understanding has been shattered into a thou-sand pieces by a malevolent reality called Legion, a synonym for im-perial Rome. Like so many victims of violence, he ruthlessly victim-izes his very self. In a futile attempt to excoriate the evil that has taken over his self-consciousness, he mutilates his own body in a vain attempt to achieve inner peace. Nothing and no one can control

the violent contortions that afflict him. There is, however, still a
spark of life within him, despite the unrelenting nightmares. This
impulse, a sign of God's reign, pushes him in a frightened way to
Jesus. His desire for grace makes grace possible, despite his own hesi-
tation. Jesus affirms the small spark of life left within and the demoniac experiences peace after years of torment. The woman with
the hemorrhage should have resigned herself to poverty and socio-
religious exclusion, but she too refuses to accept her fate. Despite
the diagnoses of wise physicians, she still hopes for a cure. An irre-
pressible desire for wholeness, an affirmation of her own worth and
gracefulness, compels her to touch Jesus' garment, a horrific breach
of social etiquette, as well as a source of ritual contamination for a
Jewish male. Her verve delights Jesus. He congratulates her on her
tenacity and faith. God's reign has broken in because a woman re-
fused to fall victim to the misogyny of a patriarchal society. Finally,
we have Jairus' daughter, a child of no account in a sexist culture
but one deeply loved by her father and mother. Their grief compels
Jesus to push through a taunting crowd, refute cynicism disguised
as common sense, and touch a corpse with all this entails in a culture
fixated on ritual purity. Jesus and the child's parents are channels of
God's uncanny grace. Their courage and compassion turn death
into life. The point of this chapter is as simple as it is demanding.
Mark invites us to be the Gerasene demoniac, the woman with a
hemorrhage, grief-stricken parents, a dead child and, ultimately, Jesus. He invites us to embody God's reign.

    When we discuss base or intentional communities it is important
to put a human face on the topic, avoiding the abstractions of so-
cial-scientific and theological jargon. Our point of reference is a
community of people who continue to hope despite their own pains
and the temptation to despair that afflicts the modern world. We are
talking about people who refuse to accept the fatalistic diagnoses of
experts about the state of the world and church. They tenaciously
pursue hope-filled solutions that change their lives and reshape the
societies they care about so intensely. The amazing fact is that there
are so many people in the Christian community who work for a
better world and defy the prophets of despair by compassionately
reaching out to human beings in need. The reign of God is very

much in our midst. Our task is the same as Mark's. We are called to understand and explain the connection between the Christian community and the reign of God.

A Strategy for Discussion

In the paragraphs that follow we will focus on three issues: the nature and task of base communities in the developing world, intentional communities in the developed world, and the common challenges both types of community face vis-à-vis their social environments and the institutional church. A distinction is being made between base and intentional communities, but the difference is not fundamental. Both are grass-roots phenomena whose purpose is the support and evangelization of their members. Both are committed to the just transformation of their respective societies. A significant difference, however, lies in the worlds they are trying to transform. Almost always, members of base communities reside in societies afflicted by class and cultural stratification with the violence such divisions produce. Members of intentional communities live in more homogenous societies, or at least in environments where inequalities and violence are more diffuse and covert. Because the latter live in the midst of visible affluence and power, these Christians are asked to challenge societies that often are blind to their own contradictions and pathology. Socio-political differences, however, do not negate similar ecclesiological assumptions and tasks. Members of base and intentional communities put great stock in mutual support and collective ability. They understand unity, holiness, Catholicity, and apostolic leadership practically rather than abstractly. Unity entails melding members in ways that lead to a vibrant, diverse community that is internally healthy and externally engaged. Holiness implies constant personal and collective reflection on how well members of the community measure up to the demands of discipleship. Catholicity means understanding the community as local reality as well as part of a larger whole that makes up Christ's body in the world. Apostolic leadership derives from a person's ability to live the gospel to its fullest and help others do the same. Leaders are people who appreciate and savor Scripture and tradition and use its wisdom to guide and teach other members of the community.

Reasoned Suspicion: The Socio-Evangelical Role of Base Communities

The emergence of base Christian communities in the 1960s is directly related to what Gustavo Gutiérrez has called the "power of the poor in history." Vatican II, Medellín, Puebla, and papal encyclicals helped, but the ultimate explanation for so much grassroots energy lies among the poor themselves, most of whom are intensely religious people. Caught up in the mid-twentieth century in the complex dynamics of modernization, they have relied on their unique language, culture, and religious wisdom to understand and respond to the larger world. The poor are not and never have been an inert mass. The rise of impersonal, capitalistic economies, along with hyper-urbanization and the decline of agrarian communities, have challenged the poor to define, organize, and celebrate their humanity in the face of dehumanizing forces. The socio-political skills of the poor are well honed. Within seconds they see through the blandishments of politicians, left and right. Highly collective in their self-understanding, they instinctively organize to defend their interests, creating structures that meet their needs. We see the results in soup kitchens, mothers' clubs, and myriad local organizations. Aware that survival requires vision, ethics, and celebration, the poor have also helped create new religious communities evident in the explosive growth of base communities. In the late sixties and early seventies, pastoral agents, aided by the insights of liberation theologians, helped these communities get off the ground. But their success is ultimately explained by the commitment of the poor themselves, people much like those we encountered in Mark's Gospel.

The challenges faced by the members of base communities are daunting. They live in societies in which in a tiny minority of powerful people systematically disregards the humanity of the majority. Many of these same societies, in Latin America and some in Africa, claim to be Christian. Their landscapes often display an abundance of Christian symbols, but their socio-economic and political systems are the antithesis of the gospel. Committed Christians in such countries are faced with a set of deadly lies. Refuting them requires prudence, knowledge, and tenacity. Specifically, Christians have to offer a reasoned critique of modernity and contemporary capitalism. They have to prove that material acquisition and exaggerated individuality are the principal sources of violence in our world today. In Pablo Richard's words, they have to refute the idols of death by living out their belief in the God of life (Richard 1983). They must point convincingly to the transcendent dimension of life to undo the numbing effects of rampant materialism. They must create healthy communities that disprove the cynical trap of exaggerated individuality that leads so many people to despair. The good news is that they have more than enough resources in their own self-understanding, culture, and religious vision. The even better news is that they are doing an effective job.

No one needs to convince the poor that developmentalism and the modernization of their societies have not worked as planned. Their daily lives are fraught with what Gramsci called "experiences of contradiction." They realize that the societies they live in are so unequal and unjust that they can never attain what they want and have been promised—reasonable security and the recognition of their humanity. Class-stratified, capitalist societies are actually poor media for real human development. Perhaps the greatest flaws in such societies is that the energy and imagination of innumerable men and women is never tapped. Driven by a sense of superiority and a primal fear of the poor as subhuman and threatening, the powerful do everything possible to silence those who see through the facade of hierarchical power and have the audacity to talk about real humanization and justice. Modern freedoms and real democracy terrify the powerful whose self-understanding and social world is predicated on controlling everyone and everything around them like so many cogs in a machine.

Disdain and oppression, however, do not silence the poor. They continue to dream and articulate an alternative vision. To use a term coined by James C. Scott, a social scientist at Yale who studies class-stratified societies, the poor develop a "hidden transcript" that calls into question the prevailing explanations of why things are the way they are. The hidden transcript is polymorphous. It takes shape in humor, song, dance, and even rituals. It is even present in popular religiosity, often disguised among layers of baroque, traditional piety. In base communities, where Christians begin to understand the truly provocative nature of Scripture and tradition, the hidden transcript becomes even more focused. Rooted in a serious analysis of the present society, the Christian transcript also relies on a vision of the future. It is both eschatological and utopic. It assesses and projects in light of its foundational vision, the reign of God.

There are three internal and interconnected activities necessary for a healthy base community capable of articulating and living its vision in a pluralistic world. Members of any community must invest a significant amount of their energy in forging strong bonds among themselves. This is a crucial element given the social and psychological pressures the poor experience in their day-to-day lives. Reading and structured reflection on Scripture is likewise crucial, using solid didactic materials and outside expertise when possible. Resonating with and understanding the human experience woven into Hebrew and Christian Scripture provides members of the community with the words, images, and values they need to understand their heritage and themselves as believing people. Finally, the members of the community must study the Catholic tradition they identify with. To capitalize on Terry Veling's insights, they must see tradition as a present reality that is actively constructed through reflective interpretation (Veling 1996). In conversation with each other, Scripture, and the Catholic tradition, members of the community grow in knowledge and confidence. They avoid self-absorption, fundamentalism, and backwards-looking religiosity. This makes them a community of psychologically balanced, intellectually reasonable Christians rather than a self-certifying, anti-rational sect.

Members of the believing community are called to explain and live out their faith in public. In societies that systematically trample on the humanity of men and women because of race, class, and gender, explaining and living out the Christian message requires articulate counterarguments and action. The Christian community must constantly pray, reflect, and act. Its praxis in the larger world assumes enormous importance. It is a palpable explanation of what the gospel means. Long-term commitment to issues like hunger, education, and human rights are crucial activities that flow from the inner core of the Christian message and self-identity of the community. Christian praxis explains the good news by doing the good news. As Juan Luis Segundo pointed out twenty years ago in his discussion of the "hermeneutic circle," praxis has a rebound effect on the community itself (Segundo 1976). It gives it ever greater insight into its own life and purpose. The meaning of Scripture as revealed and dynamic text becomes clearer as the community lives and acts in accord with its foundational documents. The Exodus and Passion narratives assume ever greater meaning as Christians connect the Hebrew people's struggle for freedom and humanity with their own. Jesus' death and resurrection are linked with their experiences of martyrdom, with the powerful example of modern disciples like Oscar Romero and other men and women who have given their lives for God's reign (Peterson 1996). The Catholic tradition becomes a living reality that dynamically links the past and present. Catholicism is understood as an incarnational way of life, a community of people who participate in God's graceful transformation of society and history. The people who form these communities contextualize and inculturate the Catholic message. By responding to the grace within them and the community as a whole, they embody and so explain central Catholic truths. They make hope real and reasonable in a world that often seems hopeless.

Intentional Communities: Christianity as Socio-Cultural Critique

Christians in the developing world who belong to intentional communities generally do not face the raw socio-economic injustice and political violence that their counterparts in the developing world confront. Nonetheless, the developed capitalist world is diseased and violent. We are dealing with societies addicted to delusions about their beneficence and virtues, whose neo-imperial economic system creates obscene affluence for a tiny elite, relative comfort for a shrinking middle class, and varying degrees of poverty for everyone else. Anesthetized by an induced naïveté, it becomes pos-

sible for the affluent to ignore the festering inner cities and the
sprawling slums of the developed and developing worlds. The pro-
ponents of late twentieth-century capitalism cannot deal with the
truth, because it is too embarrassing. The result is a socio-cultural
aversion to critical reason. Politics has devolved into glossy images
and knowledge into scientific technique. In the academic world the
very mention of values is often met with skepticism. For some, the
only value in the postmodern scheme of things is no value, a sort
of nihilistic anomie that precedes death. Christians in the developed
world have a daunting task. They have to tell the truth, reasonably
and bluntly. They must do so in societies that are terrified of public
discourse and insist that religious people and institutions vacate all
public space. Of course, to cede to these demands totally vitiates
the Christian community and message. Ethical discourse in the
form of words and praxis is imperative, not because Christians have
all the answers but because they have insights into how to live the
questions in a humane and liberating way.

Members of intentional communities also participate in an institutional church with a different history and social profile than the
church in Africa, Asia, and Latin America. Until quite recently, the
church had a large number of clergy and religious whose energy and
integrity made it a powerful social force. Despite its wariness about
modernity and its freedoms, the institutional church in many parts
of the industrial world helped people acquire the self-confidence and
skills they needed to survive and succeed in capitalist societies. It
provided people with education and firm moral criteria, finding a
niche for itself in a secular world as the guardian of tradition and
public morality. Understandably, the institutional church today has
a difficult time criticizing a socio-cultural system it has learned to
live with and in which many of its members have achieved considerable success. When the church does act prophetically it often an-
gers Catholics with a vested interest in the status quo. It raises the
hackles of liberals and conservatives, all of whom are deeply invested
in a consumption-driven capitalist system hard to reconcile with basic Christian values and the global common good.

What now complicates matters is that the institutional church
itself is in serious decline, not because of a lack of committed

people, but because the clerical system that once served it so admirably has nearly disappeared. A church based on the eucharist and a sacramental imagination has nearly run out of the clergy and religious ostensibly necessary for its survival (Greeley 1990). In many respects, the church's structural crisis is due to confusing a clerical medium with its evangelical message. It is possible to leave behind structures we no longer need. Clearly, there is no dearth of disciples today. What we need to do is create church structures that allow committed men and women in the Christian community to have a greater impact. Of course, this shift is already under way. The emergence of so many intentional communities is irrefutable proof.

Members of intentional communities are involved in an on-going hermeneutic process in which the Christian message is contextualized, that is, explained as it is lived out in the world. They do so in societies that are simultaneously skeptical of and desperate for a life-giving vision. Christians must disprove the pervasive secular assumption that their religious texts—in fact, all religious texts—are impossibly anachronistic, prescientific documents frozen in time and now devoid of meaning. They can only do this by "living" the texts, in which they demonstrate their wisdom and present-day applicability not as mere words but rather revealing insights into what it means to be human. Christians must counteract the modern assumption that believing communities are atavistic and closed, sanctuaries for people who cannot endure ambiguity and so wrap themselves in backward-looking traditions. The Catholic tradition must be explained for what it really is, a sacramental celebration of God's incarnate presence in our bodies, history, and world. In a postmodern culture in which people often view members of religious communities as fanatics that threaten individual freedoms, praxis plays an all-important role in dispelling misperceptions about Christianity and the believing community. As tolerant, accepting people involved in varied social ministries, members of intentional communities demonstrate the real nature of their beliefs and the meaning of God's reign. Doing so as neither fundamentalists nor fanatics, they give witness to the liberating message of Hebrew and Christian Scripture and the humanizing potential of a believing community's traditions. Far more important, however, is the fact that they are brothers and sisters to the shattered, the sick, and those near death, which is the ultimate reason for discipleship.

Making the Connections: Christian Communities in the Next Millennium

Base and intentional communities are reshaping Catholicism throughout the world. In a church long associated with nondemocratic governance, intellectual conservatism, and Western culture, new communities show just how agile, imaginative, and culturally diverse a two-thousand-year-old religious tradition can be. Rahner's prophetic insight about the emerging global church has come true. Diverse Catholic communities are creating a new ecclesiology that will carry the church into the future. This redefinition is not coming from on high but emerging from below. To those accustomed to a tamer sort of Catholicism, this is a disconcerting turn of events. The revitalization of the Catholic community threatens those vested in the social and ecclesiastical status quo. In egalitarian communities distinctions based on race, class, and gender quickly disappear. The cornerstones of the capitalist world are called into question. There is nothing quite as subversive as seeing someone as a sister or brother. The fact that most members of base and intentional communities are ordinary working poor or middle-class people makes them even more threatening. If they were religious sectarians or political extremists they could simply be dismissed as so many malcontents. They are, rather, normal people who function quite well in the day-to-day world. What makes them different is their refusal to worship the gods of this world—material possessions and hierarchical power.

Not surprisingly, Christian communities have their martyrs, ordinary men and women who are often nameless because they are too numerous to name. Their memory, however, is sacred and transforming. By giving their lives they have helped others realize just how precious life is. Their sacrifice helped end a civil war in El Salvador and topple a brutal dictatorship in the Philippines. Although tragic and unnecessary, their deaths prove that there is reason for hope.

Misperceptions about the socio-political nature of base and intentional communities abound. They are variously described by political conservatives as thinly disguised Marxist cells or religious splinter groups that threaten personal freedom and the secular state. The real sin of the Christian community, however, is that it dares to give voice to the voiceless. It allows people of vision from various social strata to articulate their experiences, gain insight into the real nature of their social environment, and work on behalf of the common good. Members of Christian communities effectively disprove the central premise of neoliberal thinkers and politicians who control so many countries in the world today. In the mind of this coterie of sheltered specialists economics and social policy are considered too technical for ordinary folk to understand. Gifted with superior intelligence and motivated by benevolent concern for the masses, they are better equipped to define and effect the common good, which, almost invariably, means their class-specific interests. Such arrogance impoverishes the world, literally and metaphorically. It is a sophisticated lie that has led to unprecedented poverty and class stratification in the developing world. In the developing world, neoliberal economic and social policies threaten the middle class with extinction. In the name of efficiency huge numbers of well-trained people are losing their jobs to "down-sizing." At the same time, even modest attempts to buffer people from social injustice are attacked as misguided altruism. Neoliberalism is nothing more than social Darwinism made respectable with a Ph.D. Still, people resist and envision new social arrangements that challenge the hegemony of neoliberal power brokers. The political task of Christian communities is not to engage in party politics, left or right, but rather to raise questions of conscience, born of experience and reasoned discourse about a more humane social model than the one that now controls our world. Conscientious Christians are not Luddites. They are not opposed to modernity, science, or technology. What they object to is the misuse of human resources by unscrupulous materialists who have perverted modern freedoms. The believing community does not have a pat, predetermined answer for socio-political issues, but it does have a vast amount of experience and a passionate commitment to the common good. By opting for the poor and oppressed it makes concepts like compassion, community, and the sacredness of life central to political debate in an era of ludicrous individualism and ruthless pragmatism disguised as efficient rationality.

Just as neoliberals fear religious communities with a social conscience challenging their hegemony, neoconservative groups in the church loathe base and intentional communities, which they construe as bastions of heresy. Driven by an intense need for visible structures and intellectual consistency, they deeply resent the democratization and ecclesiological diversity of the post-Vatican II church, symbolized by new forms of ecclesial community. Powerful groups like Opus Dei put enormous stress on hierarchical authority and unequivocal obedience to their definition of Catholic orthodoxy, which apparently absolves them from ever having to grapple with ambiguity. Neoconservatives long for a return to the pre-Enlightenment world, a type of kinder, gentler Christendom, albeit with the conveniences of modern technology. They equate Catholicism with the Western world and are adamant in their opposition to non-Western, nontraditional ecclesial communities. In their quest to impose order on the church and world they are willing to enter into strategic alliances with political neoliberals. Despite their differences, both groups share a fear and contempt for ordinary people and grass-roots movements. Neoconservatives in the church view men and women from the working and middle classes as unschooled victims of original sin who require hierarchical direction. What we are dealing with here is a type of neo-Augustinianism, riddled with pessimism about the human condition and the state of the modern church and world. Vatican II, with its stress on the church as People of God, and the de-Westernization of the Catholicism now in full-swing are seen as disastrous mistakes that threaten the church's integrity. What especially frightens Catholic neoconservatives about new communities is their inclusiveness and socio-political energy. Leadership that emerges from the community rather than being imposed autocratically, women and men as equal members of the community, Christians deeply involved in social change—all of this strikes them as unprecedented and even non-Catholic, despite the fact that it is an intrinsic part of the Catholic tradition, well attested throughout the church's history. Tragically, neoconservative Catholics do not celebrate the memory of Oscar Romero or María Elena Moyano, nor do they think base and intentional communities are really part of the body of Christ, despite the astounding witness and discipleship of their members.

Beyond conservative and progressive tensions within the church lies a much more significant issue. What is at stake is how we will define Catholicism in a new millennium. As Walbert Bühlmann pointed out some years ago, going well beyond Rahner's insight into Vatican II, the demographic center of Catholicism shifted decades ago from the Western, developed world to the non-Western developing world (Bühlmann 1990). Its people, with their many cultures, languages, and approaches to the sacred, are now the majority of the Catholic population. The challenge we face as members of the church is straightforward. Either we allow these people to move the Catholic tradition forward, to expand it on the basis of their humanness and faith or, de facto, we cease to be truly Catholic. This does not mean excluding Western Catholic Christians, conservative or progressive. Their insights are still perfectly valid. It does require, however, that they stop trying to control a church in which they are a minority. We cannot deny non-Western members of the church their baptismal rights without denying the incarnational, sacramental vision so central to real Catholicism. Men and women in base and intentional communities, with their non-Western and postmodern understanding of the human condition, are crucial media for evangelization in a world that needs to hear about the incarnation and experience healing grace. We must learn to celebrate ecclesiological diversity in the name of true catholicity. We have to recognize that there are many ways of being Catholic and all of them can be graced.

Not long ago, base and intentional communities would have seemed far-fetched, particularly in Catholicism. Today they are growing and reshaping Catholic Christianity in unimagined ways. The Catholic imagination survives and even flourishes where one would least expect—in peasant communities, urban slums, and even suburban parishes. Today Catholicism is becoming more Catholic, more diverse and inclusive, thanks to their commitment.

To conclude, we can return to where we began, to a tormented demoniac, the grief-stricken parents of a dying child, and a sick, bold woman. All of these people come face to face with God's reign, not as an epiphanic revelation or theological discourse, but in the person of a Gallilean Jew who embodies God's reign. Mark invites us to reach out in compassion, to offer wholeness, healing, and life. Mark is convinced that by doing so his readers can understand who Jesus is and taste God's reign. His call is being heeded by modern-day disciples in base and intentional communities, people whose commitment and compassion keep Jesus alive in our world today. As Christians we are living in a wonderful historical moment. We are finding new ways to sustain ourselves as disciples, as members of base and intentional communities that help us better explain the gospel we proclaim. Through them God's uncanny graces makes whole, heals, and gives new life. As Mark said, so should we. This is good news, our reason for hope and celebration.

References

Bühlmann, Walbert. *With Eyes to See: Church and World in the Third Millennium.* Maryknoll, N.Y.: Orbis Books, 1990.

Browning, Don S., and Francis Schüssler Fiorenza. *Habermas, Modernity, and Public Theology.* New York: Crossroad, 1992.

Cenkner, William, ed. *The Multicultural Church: A New Landscape in U.S. Theologies.* New York: Paulist Press, 1996.

Dulles, Avery, S.J. *The Catholicity of the Church.* Oxford: Clarendon Press, 1987.

Greeley, Andrew M. *The Catholic Myth: The Behavior and Beliefs of American Catholics.* New York: Scribner's, 1990.

———. *The Reshaping of Catholicism.* San Francisco: Harper & Row, 1988.

Gutiérrez, Gustavo. *The Power of the Poor in History.* Translated by Robert R. Barr. Maryknoll, N.Y.: Orbis Books, 1983.

Lee, Bernard J., and Michael Cowan. *Dangerous Memories: House Churches and Our American Story.* Kansas City, Mo.: Sheed & Ward, 1986.

Peterson, Anna L. "Religious Narratives and Political Protest." *Journal of the American Academy of Religion* 64, no. 1 (Summer 1996): 27–44.

Richard, Pablo, ed. *The Idols of Death and the God of Life: A Theology.* Translated by Barbara E. Campbell and Bonnie Shepard. Maryknoll, N.Y.: Orbis Books, 1983.

Scott, James C. *Domination and the Arts of Resistance: Hidden Transcripts.* New Haven: Yale University Press, 1990.

Segundo, Juan Luis, S.J. *The Liberation of Theology.* Translated by John Drury. Maryknoll, N.Y.: Orbis Books, 1976.

Veling, Terry A. *Living in the Margins: Intentional Communities and the Art of Interpretation.* New York: Crossroad Herder, 1996.

RESPONSE

Catherine Nerney, S.S.J.

In Curt Cadorette's homespun analysis of three significant healing events in chapter 5 of Mark's Gospel, he points to a "spark of life," a "desire for wholeness" and a "refusal of cynicism" as conditions for the further mediation of God's uncanny grace unleashed in Jesus of Nazareth in relationship with the people of his day. Cadorette chooses the Gerasene demoniac, the bent-over woman with a hemorrhage, and the dead daughter of Jairus as concrete Markan examples of the need to keep talk of Christian community concrete and personal rather than abstract and theoretical. Whether in the communities of Mark, the base communities of the developing world or the intentional communities of the developed world, "we are talking about people who refuse to accept the fatalistic diagnoses of experts about the fate of the world and church." We are talking about people who "tenaciously pursue hope-filled solutions that change their lives and reshape the societies they care about so intensely" (Cadorette). We are talking about people who have an "alternative vision" of the way life ought to be, one not derived from what the dominant culture tells them is the only way life can be. Such people in the New Testament communities and today see with the eyes of God. They compose "the church with a human face," as Edward Schillebeeckx so poignantly described it.

I have been invited to offer a "theological response" to our topic. The subject of small Christian communities engages each of us at a very personal and passionate level and to it we have committed our creative imagination, our constructive reflection, and our collective energies. My hope is to continue the conversation begun by Curt Cadorette by providing a second moment's reflection on the contemporary experience of small Christian communities. As a second moment or ecclesiological reflection, I will step back from the concrete people and the particular small Christian communities growing up and maturing throughout the world today. The movement, however, does not seek abstraction but rather enough distance to secure a longer view. My goal is to focus on certain dimensions of communion described in "Uncanny Grace" for the purpose of shedding light on the present contribution of small communities in the coming to be of a world church and their critical role in promoting a more just and compassionate future where all life can flourish in communion with divine life.

Curt Cadorette's presentation yielded creative passion and critical reasons to persuade us to attend to and rejoice in the uncanny grace and the indomitable hope at work in base and intentional Christian communities today. With appreciation for all that Curt has stirred in us, I would like to reflect further on the nature and task of small Christian communities, particularly in their role as bearers of an "alternative vision," those daring to see with the eyes of God and daring to act out of that vision. The specific lens through which I will focus my reflections will be the theological category of communion, a patristic term, retrieved by the Second Vatican Council as the primary way for understanding the nature and purpose of the Church. I will address the role of small Christian communities in helping to realize concretely the vision of the Church as communion (*koinonia*), a vision embodied in certain ecclesial elements, interiorized in certain communion attitudes and dispositions, espoused in certain communion values, lived out in certain communion behaviors and finally realized in communion structures that support and promote this fundamental relationship in both the institutional Church and the society of which it is a part.

The Church as Communion: A Vision and a Task

As a theological category, *communion* or *koinonia / communio* refers to that foundational relationship with "the God now known in Christ after Easter and through the Spirit and the community that results from *koinonia* with the Father, Son and Holy Spirit" (John H. Reumann, *Pentecost 2*, 1994, pp. 42–43). The church as a "mystery of Trinitarian communion" (*Lumen Gentium* 1,4) has kerygmatic, eucharistic, ministerial, and missionary dimensions flowing from its life in Christ and the Holy Spirit. All of these aspects of communion are addressed, more or less explicitly, in Curt Cadorette's discussion of the gift and task of base and intentional communities in today's global church and society. By reflecting on the concrete emergence of these ecclesial characteristics in small communities, one comes to marvel once again at the insight of Venerable Bede, who said, "every day the Church gives birth to the Church." The commitment to keep this symposium "close to the ground" and the study of base communities, concrete and personal, rather than abstract and theoretic, underscores the insistence of Vatican Council II that the universal church comes to be only in and through the communion of concrete, local churches (*LG* 23).

As a "mystery of Trinitarian communion," the church emerges as persons seek to understand, judge, and live their lives out of a felt response to the Spirit of God drawing them into and holding them in relationship with a community of others, who seek to live in Christ for the sake of the world. To live in Christ, through baptism, is to become a new person, a corporate person, one transformed little by little into the image that each rejects. This mystery, inexhaustibly beyond our power to explain, is unfolding in ever new and creatively diverse expressions in the barrios of Mexico City, the suburbs of Denver, the villages of Zaire, the favellas of Cochabomba, the parishes of Adelaide, Australia. In faltering yet faithful ways, many communities are discovering that they too, impelled by the same Spirit who moved in Jesus, are "Christos," God's Beloved and Anointed Ones, the Body of Christ for the world today. What are they doing with such heightened awareness? They are taking responsibility for pointing out and advancing the reign of God in human history by tirelessly "working for a better world" and tenaciously "defying the prophets of despair in their compassionate outreach to human beings in need."

In retrieving the patristic understanding of the church as a mystery of divine/human communion, rooted in the life of the Trinity, the Dogmatic Constitution on the Church, *Lumen Gentium*, has achieved a deeper understanding of the church's self-identity both for its members and for the world it seeks to serve. This self-understanding was further clarified in the pastoral constitution *The*

Church in the Modern World, (Gaudium et Spes). Here, the vision of Vatican II becomes clearer. The communion life that the church seeks to live out is not some internal cozy feeling of well-being where some specially chosen group lives peacefully removed from the struggles and conflicts of the world. In fact, the church in today's world is re-membered, re-constituted as the opening lines of that document, *Gaudium et Spes,* are emblazoned in the flesh-and-blood lives of its members.

> The joy and hope, the grief and anguish of the people of our time, especially of those who are poor or afflicted in any way, are the joy and hope, the grief and anguish of the followers of Christ, as well. Indeed, nothing that is genuinely human fails to find an echo in their hearts (*GS1*).

Clearly, the church cannot separate itself from a world radically threatened by class, race, gender, and ethnic divisions, fragmented by an isolating individualism and a utilitarian efficiency and broken in spirit by a lost sense of the transcendent, a blindness to the sacred dimensions of ordinary life. The gift of communion into which the believer is drawn in baptism and nurtured through eucharist carries the corresponding responsibility of helping to heal the world's broken communion. We all bear the theological task of seeing the "hidden wholeness" of things and bringing that graced vision to bear on a world in need.

The church realizes both its nature and its purpose when, with Thomas Merton, it understands and undertakes its painful reconciling mission of mending the broken bones of the Body of Christ (Thomas Merton, *New Seeds of Contemplation,* 1972, pp. 70–79). The church emerging within and among the base Christian communities of our global cities and villages demonstrates in new and vital ways the unifying power and demands of communion in the church's kerygma and eucharist, ministry and mission. The gifts received by the Christian communities must in turn be given both in ministry and mission. Communion in Word and Eucharist requires that communities minister to the internal needs of the *koinonia* of the community itself and move out in mission to serve the *koinonia* needs of their society.

Far from remaining abstract and indeterminate, communion manifests itself in the formational attitudes of mutual respect and fundamental trust; it is demonstrated in the reformational values of welcoming and reverencing differences, of extending and receiving forgiveness; it is lived out in the transformational behaviors of hospitality, solidarity, compassion, and reconciliation. The emergence and growth of communion attitudes, values, and behaviors lead ultimately to reshaping institutional structures to support the cumulative growth of communion living.

Core communion principles of collaboration, communication, participation, inclusivity, mutuality, and interdependence, experienced and nurtured in small communities, are unfolding new dynamic constellations of organizational life. Relationship rather than control is proving to be the authentic source of the church's inner coherence and the purpose of its life in mission. The present tensions within the church and the instability of the social order of our societies and world are directly related to the crumbling of the "old order," the patterns of isolation, domination, and exclusion that have too long characterized our Western institutions.

Rooted in the communion of the Trinity, the church emerging in small Christian communities reflects a keener sense of the interconnectedness of all living things. Particularly, with their eyes directed toward the poor, the outcast, the dying, these small Christian communities are impelled by a new vision of the world as God intends it to be. Such a thrust resonates with the eschatological vision of base Christian communities described by Curt Cadorette. As he insists, this future is not one that must await entirely God's endtime. The vision makes itself felt in the present. Like the "dangerous memory" of the Christ Event, the future vision of God's reign makes demands on the present. The result is that maturing small Christian communities, wherever they may be, are those that are coming to see the world more clearly with the eyes of God, love it with the heart of Christ, and serve it with the power of the Spirit, whose creative presence desires to heal, forgive, and welcome all into communion. This "alternative vision" and such a "hidden transcript" have already and will continue to meet unrelenting resistance from a societal vision and the powerful social systems that promote domination rather than communion, accumulation rather than sharing, autonomy rather than community, social inequity rather than the common good. In the Spirit's light, many of these base Christian communities have found and will continue to find enough illumination to look into the face of everyone they meet and recognize a brother and a sister. Such a reordering of relationships does, as Cadorette suggests, subvert the status quo and cause a shaking in the foundations of the capitalist system.

Small Communities and the Survival of Hope

Cadorette's choice of three scriptural personages from a single chapter of Mark's Gospel offers pause for further reflection as we continue the discussion on small Christian communities and their redemptive role in society. The marginalized status and vulnerable positions of these Markan figures raise disarming questions about our contemporary situation. Confronted by the Gerasene demoniac, how do we struggle to name and heal the insanity that grips our contemporary world? Standing beside the stooped and bleeding woman touching Jesus, how are we responding to the tenacious faith of many women today who refuse to accept as divinely ordained their subjugated position in both Church and society? In the company of grieving parents whose young daughter lies dead, are we crying out in rage and lament against the social conditions that threaten the lives of so many of our world's children?

In varying ways small Christian communities are providing the context for many Christians to address these and similar questions and to fashion responses to them in light of an alternative vision of wholeness and communion. To reiterate Cadorette's affirmation, the reign of God is very much in our midst.

With the current effort to name and distinguish these new experiences of the church emerging from the grass roots over the past thirty years, I found it interesting to read Cadorette's differentiation between the terms *basic* and *intentional,* a distinction he makes in light of the socio-economic context in which the two kinds of communities define their reality. Though I found the discussion of these social realities thought provoking, I am not convinced that the so-

cio-economic descriptions associated with the term *intentional* are
as normatively applicable as Cadorette seemed to indicate. My own
sense is that many small communities in the developed world no
longer "live in the midst of visible affluence and power" where "in-
equality is more covert and diffuse." More and more small community members, especially in our urban and rural settings, are becoming a part of that shrinking middle class which is recognizing itself
as one step away from a poverty imposed by an elite, privileged minority. The awareness of too gaping a gap between what Christians
see in a culture of self-serving individualism and what they believe
with eyes of faith is bringing people together for collective reassess-
ment and transformative action. Many of these people have realized,
as Curt Cadorette notes, that "survival requires vision, ethics, celebration," as evidenced in "the explosive growth of base communities."

Over the past thirty years, the worldwide grass-roots phenomena
of small Christian communities has yielded at least these two interrelated and distinct characteristics. As identified by Cadorette, small
communities are aware of an inner and outer life for which they
share responsibility. They are to provide for the support and on-going evangelization of their members and commit themselves to the
just transformation of their societies.

In attending to the inner life of the community, Cadorette speci-
fies three tasks that base Christian communities need to address. He
names: (1) the development of strong interpersonal bonds of mutual
support and life sharing; (2) the reading, reflection and on-going
formation/learning of the Hebrew and Christian Scriptures in order to understand their biblical heritage and themselves as believing
people and (3) a serious study of the Catholic tradition in which
members come to "see tradition as a present reality that is actively
constructed through their reflective interpretation."

To these essential components of the internal life of small Christian communities I will suggest two more interrelated tasks and
then briefly address each: (1) Members of small communities need
to identify with the group itself as an entity, a corporate personality,
to whom and for whom they grow in loyalty and accountability. (2)
Small communities commit themselves to serious study of "the

signs of the times," the socio-political environment that shapes them at the same time that they are called to critique, inform, and transform it.

A Corporate Identity

Members of small Christian communities experience two kinds of love. The first is a mutual bond of love for the individual members of the community and the second is love for the community itself. This second kind of loving, named "loyalty" by Josiah Royce, is an essential capacity for seeing (with the heart) the whole as well as its parts; a way of seeing that is critical to a long-term commitment to heal the world's broken communion. As Royce explained, loyalty is understood as a love for the unity of the community. In coming to an awareness of who they are as a corporate identity, small communities fashion alternative modes of being and acting in the world. They witness to the truth that an isolated Christian is no Christian (Tertullian).

Such communities create together welcoming and healing environments, spaces where silence as well as sharing are sacred, where a contemplative life stance is fostered as an alternative way of seeing the world and its daily events. Within the space created by community, transcendent values and human longing come to a more focused awareness and articulation. Prayer is experienced more simply and profoundly as an intimate relationship with the Transcendent One, the Source and End of their longing. As prayer precedes, accompanies, and follows their individual and corporate action in the outer world, the rhythm of contemplation and courageous action becomes a more coherent way of life.

Critiquing the Signs of the Times

Within the space of a nurturing community, the individuals and community grow in self-critique in light of the gospel and Catholic tradition. In turn, they become "hearers of the word" who both challenge and are challenged by the tradition they have received in faith. As embodiments of the Church's living tradition, they hand on, "all that the Church is and all that the Church believes" (*Dei Verbum* 8). They emerge as the new bearers of faith's flame, "the spark of life" still burning through the ages. This responsibility for "passing on the flame" becomes for small Christian communities a genuine expression of "apostolic succession," bringing to bear the faith of the apostles on this, their time in salvation history. From that living flame of faith, the invincible power of love—even in situations brimming with hatred—is charged and the survival of hope in a world failing prey to despair is assured.

Both in the developed world and in the developing worlds, communities are fashioning a "hidden transcript," an alternative to the "narrative of the lie" which would have us believe that materialism, productivity, and efficiency measure the genuine worth of human persons and the societies they construct. As Cadorette pointed out, where these base communities are formulating their "hidden transcripts" in light of the provocative and, I would add, even subversive message of the gospel, the narrative of liberating love carries power to decry and expose the prevailing story of human domination and oppression. As small Christian communities embody "the Church with a human face," they likewise give the Church its public face. The Christian community does not and has never existed except in and for mission, its role is to be in and for the world as agents of God's reconciling presence and action in Christ through the Spirit. In small Christian communities, "explain the good news by living the good news" is the persuasive description of Christian praxis offered by Curt Cadorette.

Understanding action on behalf of justice as a constitutive element of the gospel is core to the self-identity of many of the small Christian communities developing in our present day. This ecclesiological principle, expressed by the bishops of the United States in 1971, has proven credible and transformative because it is first and foremost a reflection on sustained praxis rather than an abstract theory to be tested. By embodying their foundational documents, small Christian communities are becoming communities of the Living Word of God. In the dying and rising of their eucharistic lives, small Christian communities are becoming the Body of Christ that they receive.

The genetic process by which the Church is born anew consists of a mutual exchange. A contemporary group of people through the life-giving work of the Spirit becomes both the active and responsible subject (the subjective pole of the Church) as well as the active and graced recipient of the Church's tradition (the objective pole of the Church). In receiving the Christian story, the community inherits more than a rich past; it receives a message with a future intent, what Johann Metz calls the Church's dangerous memory, alive with the potential to make future demands on its hearers. Likewise, when Christian communities claim for themselves the "sacramental imagination" of the Catholic heritage, they dare to see more than what appears. They know at a deeper level that ordinary human life is holy. The catholic vision culminates when its bearers recognize the face of God in the disfigured guise of our earth family's poorest ones.

In giving itself over to the Word (the *kerygma*) and in the mutual interchange that is the eucharist, each vibrant community of faith, one by one, births the Church again. In communion with the Church catholic, present throughout time and across space, small Christian communities in Africa, in El Salvador, in Chicago testify to the truth that there is no universal Church except in its concrete universality, the one Catholic Church in its many diverse and particular manifestations. The Church of the next millenium grows now in our midst. Growing numbers of small Christian communities continue to ignite the same "spark of life," to nurture the same "desire for wholeness" and to sustain the same "refusal of cynicism" that mediated the healing presence of Christ in the Markan text, interpreted so fruitfully by Curt Cadorette for our discussion. There is, indeed, cause for rejoicing here, not because the social structures of our Church and societies are dissipating, but because out of their dying, new life is emerging in forms, such as small Christian communities.

The presence and action of small Christian communities growing and maturing throughout our world reflect in human history a closer resemblance to the organic nature of all life forms. New patterns of order emerging out of ecclesial chaos testify to the dynamic character of all life, newly discovered by astronauts and physicists, experientially known and attested to by mystics and saints for centuries and preserved in the most genuine doctrines of the Church's tradition. The contemporary scientific and cosmological vision of life sees the whole of creation flowing out of and being embraced by an interconnected web of relationships where unity and diversity flourish simultaneously.

The Christian vision sees in this dynamic pattern the mystery of Trinitarian Communion, where all creation is held in a divine unity of infinite variety. Christians are challenged to bring this "alternative vision" to bear on the shape of human history. The survival of our hope rests in God alone, whose uncanny grace has offered us sufficient reason to believe that small Christian communities are commissioned to be architects of this new social order for the third millenium.

RESPONSE

Alicia Butkiewicz

The SCCs started in Bolivia in the early 1970s. The situation—social, political, and economic—was such that people needed to organize. This was really a need for the poor people because of their poverty. We began with groups sharing Bible reflections, mothers' clubs, and other small groups. An important factor that really helped this experience of small Christian communities was the support coming from our bishops. We have so many documents—one is from 1987—where they speak about the need to organize basic Christian communities. The bishops looked at the reality of the Bolivian situation and in this early document explained that it was a new model for living the Christian experience and it was an answer for the people.

The organization really grew because of the priests, sisters and lay people who have this new vision of the Church—that it has to change to answer the needs of the poor. It is true that some priests and sisters didn't actively support these documents, but for those of us working in the movement it was a great support.

Challenges to the Bolivian SCCs

Now the questions are different than before. One very important item is formation. It is necessary now to form in the people a critical conscience. In Bolivia we are going through so many changes. I don't know who understands them. For example, there is to be a major change in education. They are proposing popular participation. What will capitalization of the economy mean? What will be the impact of these changes on the poor? Some of our people are wary because they know that in the past they have been manipulated by the politicians. They don't want that any more. They want to understand and have a voice in how things are done. That is why it is essential to provide for them a formation in a critical conscience. They want it and we are trying to provide it. The small Christian communities are a good forum for this social awareness. This is really our biggest challenge, I think.

Another challenge facing us is how to integrate popular movements with evangelical values. This government is offering popular movements, you know, almost parallels to the SCCs. Again, the people don't want to be manipulated and they want to understand exactly what the government is proposing. Our people are now aware that we are involved so much in ecclesial issues. We need to go more into social issues. But we are looking for leadership in these matters from people with Christian values who can help us through all these changes as a Bolivian people.

A third thing is that people in the SCCs want to change from being a kind of charitable support of different causes (this is easy to do), and turn more toward the fight for justice and our rights. Here is a key issue and one in which we have a problem. Sometimes there is a big clash between the formation of the clergy in the seminaries, where there is still a hierarchical understanding, and the formation of the lay people, who are more apt to understand participation. It is a challenge as to how we can help the priests realize what we are going through as small Christian communities.

Signs of Hope

I think the one thing that I see as most important is the clearer respect for the poor. Now they have more than just "themselves" to give us—they can talk and think and help not only the Church but our country, our reality. That is a big "sign of hope" for me.

Another big hope is seen in the participation of the laity in the Church. The people now know that the Church is not just the clergy, it is not just the priests and sisters with we lay people taking a back seat in the Church. Now the laity are very active. The people are building Church!

Another thing is the presence of the Church in the poor neighborhoods, in the rural areas, and in the mines. It moves both ways—

the Church is present in these poor places and at the same time the poor are present in the Church.

A further sign of hope is the presence and role of women in the Church. You know that Latin America is known as a "macho" culture. But, in fact, for us now, who are the protagonists in social issues, in the Church, in any place? The women! It is so nice to see poor women who formerly were considered nothing and now know that they have real value. The same is true for the campesinos. So many people moving from the rural areas to the cities now have a sense of belonging to the Church and to a group. That is a big sign of hope.

We realize in the SCCs we are not alone. We are with God and with so many people who are now asking what we think, what we experience. In our communities we now are becoming the Church in embryo!

SMALL CHRISTIAN COMMUNITIES IN THE CATHOLIC CHURCH

A Study in Progress

William D'Antonio

My interest in small Christian communities as a social movement is an outgrowth of my participation in a particular type of SCC from 1984 to the present. This particular SCC is known as an Intentional Eucharistic Community, and the one I am a member of in Washington, D.C., is called simply Communitas. The story of how it came into being helps us to understand one kind of SCC in the U.S.A. and provides a point along a continuum that identifies a range of beliefs and practices among American Roman Catholics.

I had arrived in Washington, D.C., in August 1982 as Executive Officer of the American Sociological Association, on a leave of absence from the University of Connecticut. Since our two youngest daughters were still in college, my wife thought it best that she remain at our home in Connecticut, so we took turns commuting between D.C. and Tolland, Connecticut.

I had gone to Mass at the Newman Center of George Washington University with colleagues who taught there, and found myself very comfortable with the liturgy, its dialogue homily and strong feminine influence. So I made that my away from home parish, and gradually became acquainted with some of the fifty or sixty regular attendees.

Sometime in early 1984 a new pastor was assigned to Newman, and he strongly objected to the presence of women at the altar, or reading the Gospel, or giving homilies. There was a confrontation, followed by a series of meetings held by the long-time members of that particular liturgy group, and the decision to break with Newman rather than accede to the pastor's demands to return to a more traditional eucharistic celebration. Some fifty or sixty people organized a "pilgrim church," found several priests willing to say Mass with them, and found a Presbyterian church that offered them a room to worship in for several months. I joined the group which decided to call itself Communitas. After several months in "the room," we found a room at the local YWCA, where we formally organized and late in 1984 advertised for and hired a pastoral minister to oversee the various activities of our community. By that time we had several priests who regularly celebrated with us. We soon developed a formal mission statement, a constitution and by-laws, a council, and a series of committees to help us run our parish/community.

Over time, of course, there have been changes in the membership body, with newcomers, people moving away, and a gradual aging of the membership. As of the most recent parish membership list, we have about fifty-four active members, another fifty friends, very few young people, and still five or six priests who celebrate with us on a rotating basis. We now meet for liturgy on Sundays at 10 A.M. in the International Youth Hostel in downtown Washington. We also meet at other times on a wide range of topics and issues. Addressing structural issues in matters of church and civil society are a major concern of many members.

In 1990 under the leadership and inspiration of our pastoral minister, we began discussions on the growth of small faith communities in several parts of the world, especially Africa, Europe, and Latin America. And we sponsored our pastoral minister to a number of national and international conferences.

Soon thereafter, she proposed that we think about holding a consultation of our own, inviting to Washington members of other Intentional Eucharistic Communities(IECs). With the assistance of leaders of several neighboring IECs, we began to build a national list of IECS. Some fifteen or sixteen IECs sent representatives to D.C. for a three-day gathering in May 1991. Each IEC presented a written history, statement of mission, and vision for the future church. As I listened to the people who had come from just about all regions of the country and read their materials, I began to think of IECs in a new light, as possibly signaling a new social movement within the Church.

At about the same time two academic colleagues, Nancy Ammerman and Clark Roof, invited me to write an article for a book they were editing on *Work, Family, and Religion*. I agreed to do so, motivated in part by a growing realization that people within the IECs seemed particularly committed to making their religion relevant to work and family. The article is titled "Small Faith Communities in the Roman Catholic Church: New Approaches to Religion, Work and Family." The book was published by Routledge in 1995.

In that article I devoted considerable space to the Christian Family Movement as a precursor to current efforts to challenge Catholics to bring their religion alive in work and family relations. In this vein I referred to the work of Father, later Cardinal, Joseph Cardijn as the original source for the ideas that undergird these movements, with his focus on "Observe, Judge, and Act." I also included some descriptive information on Buena Vista, RENEW, the North American Forum on Small Christian Communities and Father Art Baranowski's National Alliance of Parishes Restructuring into Communities. But most of my attention was on the Intentional Eucharistic Communities as seen through the documents and notes taken during the 1991 gathering. I began to see myself not simply as a member of a small group of Catholics trying to survive inside the Church, but as possibly part of a new and dynamic social movement that might help transform the Church.

The writing of this article coincided with an invitation to a March 1992 Conference on Small Christian Communities in New Orleans, organized by Bernard Lee. At that gathering I met leaders from BV, NAF, and NAPRC, and they provided me vital new information and ideas for the paper I was then writing. More important, through Bernard Lee's ideas and prodding I began to see the possibility of a national study of SCCs as a large and complex social movement. Still, I was sufficiently preoccupied with the laity book that was then in progress, so I let the idea of a study develop slowly in my mind.

The SCC Project

In the spring of 1994, Bernard Lee called, inviting me to join him in a joint sociological/theological study of SCCs and to seek funds from the Lilly Foundation. In the late fall of 1994 Lilly provided funds for a pilot project to carry out a census of SCCs in the Catholic Church in the United States. The census was designed to determine the extent, intensity, types, and basic demographic characteristics of SCCs in the U.S. Roman Catholic Church. Included in the survey was a question designed to ascertain what things SCC members did when they met. We will look closely at the data from that question later in this paper. This census was actually completed in the spring of 1996, even as we began the second phase of our study. I will present some tables from the census later.

Suffice it to say that the Lilly Foundation was impressed with the rich array of data we were gathering, showing that SCCs were to be found in all parts of the country, that there were a range of SCCs to be found, and that they were showing both dynamic new growth and considerable stability over time. The result was that the new proposal prepared by Bernard Lee was funded for two full years, 1996 and 1997, allowing us to fulfill a number of objectives.

In the present stage, which began in March 1996 and will be completed in December 1997, we set the following objectives:

1. A comparative study of U.S. adult Catholics, both those who do and who not belong to SCCs, and former Catholics, focused on their values, beliefs, and behavior. The comparative analysis is designed to probe whether SCC members differ in significant ways in their values, beliefs, and behavior from non-SCC Catholics. A subquestion has to do with ex-Catholics or former Catholics. What may have caused them to leave the Church and how may their values and beliefs differ from those of the other two groups? Our survey should help us learn more about who becomes an ex-Catholic, why they drop out, and whether they join other religious denominations. Thus, we expect to be able to compare Catholics with ex-Catholics and both with SCC Catholics. A fundamental question is what difference it makes in attitudes, beliefs, values, and behavior whether

one is a SCC member, a Catholic in the pews, or an ex-Catholic who may or may not be a member now of another denomination.

To obtain this information, we are using a multi-stage methodology. The national representative sample of Roman Catholics and ex-Catholics is being obtained by use of the telephone polling method known as random digit dialing. The sample size is 800, and the University of Maryland Survey Research Center is carrying out the study for us. It is expected that some 20 percent of the sample will be ex-Catholics, based on surveys carried out in recent years by Gallup and the National Opinion Research Center of Chicago. Because we do not expect to find a sufficient number of SCC members in the national survey, we are drawing samples of SCC members from the six major types of SCCs we have identified and are mailing them the same questionnaire. These samples are designed also to be representative of the whole body of SCC members. We expect the data-gathering to be completed by late December.

2. We are also currently in the process of mailing a questionnaire to a representative sample of SCC members designed to learn what motivated them to join SCCs and how their membership in SCCs has affected their lives, their beliefs, and their values. This study involves a comparative analysis of the six major types of SCCs to see if there are ways in which these several types vary or differ regarding motivation and behavior. The mailing will be sent to about 2,500 SCC members, with the expectation that we will receive a 50 percent response. We have used the telephone to contact SCC leaders to insure their cooperation. We hope to have the mailing completed by mid-November and the data ready to be analyzed by mid-January 1997.

3. The final data-gathering involves an intensive participant observation study of some thirty to thirty-five SCCs, designed to help us better understand how SCCs operate, how members interact, and how SCCs may be distinguished from each other by their meeting patterns. Again, we will sample across the several major types of SCCs.

I expect we will be going into the field in March or April and that researchers will spend four to seven days with a parish or group or a particular area, depending on the density and intensity of activity.

A Brief Demographic Portrait of SCCs in the U.S.A.

A word about the range and nature of the SCCs we have uncovered in our study. I will use a number of tables to provide some of the information we gathered in the census stage of our study.

The first thing I would like to have you focus on in table 1 is the range in types of SCCs we are working with. We have identified six major types, the first of which we identify here with the letters SC. SC refers to a generic type into which we fit the major national organizations: Buena Vista, the North American Forum, the National Alliance of Parishes Restructuring into Communities (NAPRC), and NCR (National Catholic Reporter).

Several words of explanation are due here. In order to reach out to SCCs that might be fairly autonomous, that is, not formally affiliated with a diocesan recognized parish or with the North American Forum, Buena Vista, or NAPRC, we included notices in the *National Catholic Reporter* newspaper and the *Call To Action* newsletter. We asked readers who were members of SCCs to fill out the form attached to the notice and mail to us. We received more than a hundred responses to the *NCR* notice and about twenty-five more from *CTA* readers. It turned out that a majority of the *NCR* respondents were members of SCCs that emerged out of RENEW (not directly sampled in this first stage), BV, NAF, or NAPRC. Their responses also were so similar to the others that we included them in this generic type. A smaller number of NCR respondents identified themselves as members of groups that were clearly of the IEC type, that is, met regularly and included eucharistic celebrations as one of their central actions. They were added to the IEC type.

You will note that CTA is shown here as a separate type. Again, some of the respondents who sent in the form that had been in the CTA newsletter were found to be members of the generic SC type, but others were not. In addition, we examined the CTA Directory from the 1995 Chicago meeting and decided to send census questionnaires to all CTAs that identified themselves as SCCs. When we examined their responses, we found them sufficiently distinctive on a couple of variables that we decided to make them into a separate SCC type.

Ch refers to Charismatic prayer groups. The director of Charis-center read our notice in NCR and sent us a letter urging that the Charismatic prayer groups be included in the study. I met with Walter Mathews, the director; then Bernard Lee and I reviewed the materials they had sent us, and we decided that we should include them, since it was clear that in some basic ways they seemed to fit the very broad model of SCCs as we were thinking of them.

As should be clear now, we had decided to cast a very large net and allow groups to identify as SCCs as they chose. This enabled us to learn what beliefs and practices Catholics themselves identified as being constitutive of SCCs.

CM refers to SCCs resulting from campus ministry efforts. I had been very uncertain about the value of including CM in the study, but Bernard Lee convinced me, and while this type is small and much less stable than the others, it may well become an important source of recruitment of young people into the movement in the twenty-first century. We found evidence of SCCs on about forty college campuses, and that number has grown during the course of this year's work. Indeed, the growth of SCCs on college campuses, Catholic and secular, may be one of the more dynamic features of the SCC movement today. We will know more in another few months.

HM refers to the Hispanic ministry. Many of you know that as far back as 1987 the American bishops announced an intention of supporting the growth of SCCs within the Hispanic ministry. But even before their decision, there was work already afoot within Hispanic areas of the Southeast and Southwest to build SCCs, both using the model of Comunidades de Base, SINE from Mexico, and variants of RENEW and other American models. Thus, for example, there were between four and five hundred SCCs in the Browns-ville diocese by 1990, mostly due to the support given by its bishop. In January of this year, the bishops formally approved a plan for the formation of SCCs within the Hispanic ministry, with Ron Cruz of NCCB as overall director. Ideally, there will be a person in charge of HM in every diocese with a significant number of Hispanics; for now the goal is 150 dioceses. A problem is that these people will be in charge of all phases of the HM within the diocese, so SCC activity will vary greatly, depending on the time, energy, knowledge about and attitude towards SCCs. We have found SCCs within the Hispanic populations in almost all parts of the country. Hispanics are proving to be an interesting variant on the SCC models.

The IECs are the Intentional Eucharistic Communities that have been created largely by lay people who invite clergy to celebrate with them. In 1991 we were able to identify some sixteen or seventeen. We now have more than fifty in this category.

You will note that RENEW was not included in this first stage of our study. We had available from the national office of RENEW in New Jersey, a great amount of information about RENEW, and did not feel we needed to do a census of RENEW groups at that stage. Both the officials at RENEW and Professor James Kelly of Fordham, in his study of RENEW, concluded that some three to four million Americans had taken part in RENEW since its inauguration in 1979–80. Besides, we had already learned that BV and NAF, in particular, work closely with RENEW. Clearly, RENEW has been the single most important force in the SCC movement in the U.S. in the last fifteen years. RENEW programs have been carried out in two out of three U.S. dioceses now (some 124 of the 186 officially listed).

Since the beginning of this year RENEW groups have become a central part of our study. Under the leadership of Msgr. Tom Kleisler and Sister Mary McGuinness, RENEW has begun to move into its next phase, called appropriately enough Post-RENEW. The mission of Post-RENEW is to enlarge the vision of the laity to see the need for outreach (good deeds as well as structural reform) as at the core of Jesus' teachings.

As an aside, there are a number of other SCC types not included here, but which are a part of our larger study. I mention them briefly, in case some of you may be wondering about them:

— The St. Boniface Church cell system, in Pembroke Pines, Florida, derived from a cell model developed by Pastor Paul Cho, of an Assembly of God church in Seoul, South Korea. His church has fifty thousand members, but he prefers to think of the congregation belonging to thousands of small cells. St. Boniface claims to be modeled on Pastor Cho's church, with 550 parishioners in some forty cells meeting regularly in homes throughout the parish. The cell idea has become popular in the growing number of megachurches in the U.S.A. A recent issue of the *Atlantic Monthly* (October 1996) provides an up-to-date analysis of the use of cells (small groups) in megachurches. One such church claims six hundred "Tender Loving Care" groups of eight to ten families in each. (See chap. 4, "How Small Groups Shape an Apostolic People," in *Church for the Unchurched*, by George G. Hunter III, 1996, Abingdon Press).

— The Christian Life Communities, formerly the Jesuit Sodality movement, rapidly being transformed into modern-day SCCs. Some sixty-four are known to be active in the U.S.A.

— Teams of Our Lady, a small faith type limited to married couples which originated in France in post–WWII, with a charter from the Vatican. In the U.S. there are some five thousand married couples. Whether or not it will ultimately meet more rigid criteria to qualify as an SCC type, we have included it for now.

— I mentioned SINE briefly before; I am aware that Father Navarro has been giving workshops in various parts of the U.S. in recent years, but so far we have not turned up enough SCCs of this type to include them in our study as a separate type.

— We have heard from a number of parishes where the pastor and parishioners are working together to create their own version of a cell or small group system. We are collecting information on these parishes in a separate file.

— Finally, we are gathering data on SCCs within religious orders, especially single-sex (mostly women) SCCs. It is too early to say much about this type, but they are beginning to become visible to us.

I return now to the demographic data from our census study; table 1: If we limit the size of SCCs to adults, we find the range from twelve to fifty, with women typically outnumbering men, by two to one ratios in the smaller SCCs, but only slightly in the IECs and on campus.

Table 1: Average Number of Persons in SCCs by Gender and SCC Type.

	SC[1]	CTA[2]	CH[3]	CM[4]	HM[5]	IEC[6]
Men	4	5	11	11	3	27
Women	8	10	18	14	9	33
Under 18	1	1	4	1	4	19
N	405	77	91	22	97	46

1. SC (Buena Vista, NAFR, NAPRC, NCR)
2. CTA (Call To Action)
3. CH (Charistmatics)
4. CM (Campus Ministry)
5. HM (Hispanic Ministry)
6. IEC (Intentional Eucharistic Communities).

Table 2: Percent of SCCs Meeting Weekly, Biweekly, and So Forth by SCC Type.

	SC %	CTA %	CH %	CM %	HM %	IEC %
Weekly	37.3	21.0	79.1	78.3	81.4	60.4
Biweekly	38.1	42.0	13.2	4.3	15.5	22.9
Every 3 weeks	2.0	1.2	1.1			
Monthly	13.0	28.4	4.4	13.0	3.1	6.3
Other	9.5	7.4	2.2	4.3		10.4
N	405	77	91	22	97	46

Table 2 shows that the great majority of all SCCs meet at least every other week, with 60 to 80 percent of four of them actually meeting every week. This is a very positive sign for us, as our own vision of what an SCC should be like includes regular meetings, more often than monthly. We will discuss this variable at some length at a later stage of our study.

Table 3 shows that with the exception of the Charismatics and the students, the great majority of SCCs meet away from a parish building. How important that is for the autonomy of the group remains to be examined.

One of our main concerns has to do with the longevity of SCCs; are they perhaps just another fad, doomed to disappear shortly? Or

Table 3: SCCs Meeting Place, by SCC Type.

	SC %	CTA %	CH %	CM %	HM %	IEC %
Member's Home	71.7	75.7	31.6	20.8	85.4	75.6
Public Building	3.2	4.1	1.1		1.8	10.8
Parish Building	25.1	20.2	66.3	29.2	12.8	13.6
Campus Ministry Office				50.0		
N	405	77	91	22	97	46

Table 4: SCCs Longevity, by SCC Type.

	SC %	CTA %	CH %	CM %	HM %	IEC %
Less Than One Year	11.1	12.2	3.3	30.4	8.0	6.3
1–3 Years	40.1	36.6	15.2	26.1	30.7	14.6
4–5 Years	22.0	14.6	12.0	8.7	31.8	4.2
6–10 Years	18.4	17.1	19.6	8.7	14.8	27.1
11–20 Years	6.8	14.6	23.9	4.3	10.2	18.8
21- Years	1.6	4.9	26.1	21.7	4.5	29.2
N	405	77	91	22	97	46

is there evidence of real staying power? Table 4 shows the Charismatics and the IECs to have substantial staying power, with half or more having been in existence for eleven or more years. Since they seem to reflect opposite ends of a traditional/progressive orientation to the Church, that makes the finding even more interesting. This table also shows us the dynamic quality of SCCs, with large percentages of the SC, CTA, CH, and HM types having been in existence three years or less. Overall, the SCCs seem to demonstrate both dynamic growth and considerable staying power.

Table 5 shows the activities SCCs engage in when they gather. The most common activities across types are prayer, faith sharing, reading and discussion of the Scriptures, and spirituality. Not surprisingly, students and the IEC members share Eucharist at every meeting.

One of our central concerns was, and is, to what extent do SCCs address structural issues of Church and civil society? There are only

Table 5: Activities SCCs Engage In at Every Meeting by SCC Type.

	SC %	CTA %	CH %	CM %	HM %	IEC %
Prayer	89.7	88.9	100.0	95.7	99.0	81.3
Faith Sharing	83.1	86.3	85.1	63.6	84.2	55.3
Read/Discuss						
Scripture	75.5	72.5	73.9	43.5	97.9	64.6
Spirituality	65.7	68.5	77.8	78.3	70.9	56.5
Group Silence	41.3	44.9	62.2	22.7	43.9	16.3
Weekend Eucharist	31.1	20.3	30.8	56.5	40.0	78.3
Theological Reflection	26.6	36.4	13.3	27.3	28.6	34.8
Helping Members	26.1	22.7	18.4	22.7	33.0	23.4
Sharing Visions	24.3	31.6	21.3	9.1	25.6	29.5
Helping in Need	16.4	19.7	12.4	18.2	23.3	25.5
Evangelization	11.5	6.1	29.5	4.5	49.4	2.4
Home Eucharist	5.8	11.6	6.1	8.7	3.7	28.3
Issues	8.0	26.0	3.6	4.3	25.0	19.6
N	405	77	91	22	97	46

Table 6: Percentages of SCC Members at Various Age Levels, by SCC Type.

	SC %	CTA %	CH %	CM %	HM %	IEC %
> 18	7.5	2.48	19.87	5.34	24.32	25.47
18–29	3.7	4.11	4.39	74.01	8.42	9.03
30–39	12.07	15.75	12.84	7.23	14.25	15.12
40–49	24.41	26.03	19.04	3.44	19.55	19.67
50–59	25.03	26.37	22.36	3.61	16.17	16.90
60–69	20.57	18.41	15.19	4.65	13.45	9.30
70 >	6.80	6.85	6.30	1.72	3.84	4.52
N	4458	1168	2048	581	1509	3498

three types (CTA, Hispanics, and the IEC) where 20 percent or more of the groups address these issues regularly. When we get to the participant observation part of our research we will get a better feel for how these three and the other types actually try to address these issues.

Table 7: The Educational Level of SCCs, by SCC Type.

	SC %	CTA %	CH %	CM %	HM %	IEC %
High School Graduates or Less	20.38	13.46	31.40	4.13	68.44	12.85
Some College	25.42	14.14	24.15	56.78	12.11	19.67
College Graduates	31.66	39.47	29.40	16.61	11.83	34.17
Graduate and Professional Degrees	22.65	32.91	15.11	22.48	7.97	32.70
N	405	77	91	22	97	46

Table 8: The Racial/Ethnic composition of SCCs by SCC Type.

	SC %	CTA %	CH %	CM %	HM %	IEC %
African American	1.68	1.66	3.88	0.80	0.03	0.90
Asian American	1.30	0.48	5.71	3.05	0.03	0.52
Hispanic/Latino	6.80	1.86	13.70	7.75	95.38	5.42
Native American	0.42	0.40	3.00	0.00	0.54	0.06
White	89.81	95.51	75.23	88.40	3.41	91.33
N	405	77	91	22	97	46

Regarding the ages of SCC members, table 6 shows both the range of ages, and the fact that the great majority of SCC members are forty or older. Indeed, the average age of the general SCC type, which is the largest single type, is closer to sixty than to forty. IECs and the Hispanics have the largest percentages of young people, probably reflecting the eucharistic nature of the IECs, thus the family to church tie, and the more traditional family-oriented nature of the Hispanic SCCs. The newly married and those with young children are not as likely to be drawn to SCCs, with the exceptions I just noted.

Table 7 reveals another important fact about SCC members, how well-educated they are. Only among Hispanics do we find a majority without at least some college, and only among the Charismatics do we find a majority without a college degree. People who are attracted to SCCs are highly educated Catholics, with as many as one in three holding graduate and professional degrees. Overall, these figures suggest that SCC types attract members over the broad range of the Catholic population.

Table 8 shows that there is some African American and Asian American representation among all the SCC types, which is also true for the Hispanics. Still, the overwhelming majority of all SCC members are white. The Charismatics are the most likely to have the broadest representation of racial/ethnic types. So far, we have found only two African American parishes in the U.S. with SCCs.

Possible Larger Significance of This Study

I close on a most optimistic note. Our study follows and builds upon the work of Robert Wuthnow of Princeton, whose recent book *Sharing the Journey* (Free Press, 1994) helped draw attention to the growing phenomenon of small faith groups in the U.S.A. Wuthnow found that forty percent of all Americans said they belonged to a small group, and that almost 60 percent of those were related to a church or other faith community.

In his 1996 Report on Religion in America, Gallup noted that while Wuthnow found that many groups fostered an "anything goes" spirituality, others both challenged and comforted their members, "helped people in their faith journey, and encouraged them to be open and honest with each other." Further, said Gallup, "small groups can serve as both a support for persons who find the church setting too impersonal, as well as an entrance to the larger community. The growth of these groups, involving close to half the populace, and the intense searching for spiritual moorings suggest that a widespread healing process may be under way in our society. Because most Americans believe in a personal, approachable God . . . we are predisposed to reach out in this direction for guidance."

Gallup concluded with these reflections:

> When functioning at a deep spiritual level, small groups can be the vehicle for changing church life from the merely functional to the transformational. The development of small groups of this nature . . . can help meet two of the great desires in the hearts of Ameri-

cans, particularly at this point in time: the desire to find deeper meaning in our world, and the desire to build deeper, more trusting relations with other people in our often impersonal and fragmented society. If these desires are sincerely and creatively addressed, the vitality of America's churches could well be the surprise of the next century. ("Religion in America." 1996 Report. Princeton Religion Research Center, pp. 11–12)

Our study of small Christian communities in the U.S. Catholic Church supports Gallup's contention that these small groups may well play a vital role in shaping our society in the century that will soon be upon us.

THE EVOLVING SOCIOLOGY
AND ECCLESIOLOGY OF CHURCH
AS FAMILY IN EASTERN AFRICA

East African participants in the consultation

Five people from East Africa, including Mrs. Rose Musimba and Father Joe Healey, participated in the International Consultation on Christian base communities at the University of Notre Dame, Indiana, U.S.A., in December 1991. Now almost five years have passed. Our countries of Kenya, Tanzania, and Uganda are different. Our small Christian communities are different. Among the most notable changes have been the rapid increase of urbanization and the democratized/multi-party political process. Among the most significant events have been the 1994 African Synod and its initial implementation since Pope John Paul II's visit to Nairobi, Kenya in September 1995 and the proclamation of the final document, the Post-Synodal Apostolic Exhortation *The Church in Africa*. As we gather for another international consultation and take a new step in the development of small Christian communities as a "New Way of Being Church," we share with you some of our recent experiences and reflections.*

I. Case Studies of Small Christian Communities in Nakuru and Nairobi, Kenya

Cathedral Church of Christ the King in Nakuru Town, Kenya

The Cathedral Parish of Nakuru Diocese in Kenya is composed

*This paper was presented by Rev. Joseph Healey, M.M. (Tanzania), Mrs. Rose Musimba (Kenya), Archbishop Raphael Ndingi Mwana'a Nzeki (Kenya), Rev. Aylward Shorter, M.Afr. (Kenya) and Rev. John Mary Waliggo (Uganda).

of thirteen Small Christian Communities (SCCs). The Cathedral
Mass Center comprises six SCCs. This includes St. Catherine of
Siena's Center (previously a single SCC) which grew so large that it
divided into two SCCs: St. Stephen SCC and St. Theresa of the
Child Jesus SCC following the neighborhood street plan ("mitaa")
of urban Nakuru. From 6 p.m. to 7:40 p.m. on Tuesday, 4 June
1996, Archbishop Raphael Ndingi and Father Joe Healey participated in a joint gathering of these two SCCs which was a kind of
prayer meeting using the format of Evening Prayers in Swahili. The
Bible passage was a section on "Love" from I Corinthians.

Hekima Mass Center comprises four SCCs which meet on Sunday
afternoon (in the church to show the unity of all the SCCs together)
and Tuesday and Thursday evenings (in individual homes of Christians). From 6:15 p.m. to 8 p.m on Thursday, 6 June 1996, Archbishop Raphael Ndingi and Father Joe Healey participated in a joint
gathering of St. Michael SCC and St. Elizabeth SCC. The format
was similar to the Tuesday gathering above. The Bible passage was
a section on "Victory in Christ" from II Corinthians.

Sometimes due to large numbers St. Elizabeth SCC divides into
as many as four different prayer groups in the individual homes of
Christians. Another community is St. Peter SCC, which might have
twenty members at one meeting. Activities of the SCCs include
celebrations such as baptisms and weddings, visiting the sick and
raising funds for specific projects such as helping the poor at Christ-
mas. Requests for the baptism of children pass through the SCCs.

Both prayer meetings included a lot of popular Catholic religiosity such as the rosary with extra devotional prayers, litanies, and
spiritual ejaculations in the Bible reflections. This is clearly where
many of the local Kenyan people are at in their popular piety. The
Prayers of the Faithful in Swahili were rather traditional and general. Had they been in the local Kenyan languages such as Kikuyu
and Kamba they would have been more expressive of the real spirituality and felt needs of the people. The individual reflections on
the Bible were too long (as much as five minutes) and were like little
sermons or exhortations on the Scriptures rather than looking at
our daily lives in light of the Bible and looking at the Bible in light
of our daily lives.

In both gatherings there was a lot of enthusiasm and a good spirit. The welcome, the singing, the tea and rolls and the dancing goodbyes radiated a joyful spirit.

Section of Mukuru Catholic Parish in Nairobi, Kenya

Mukuru (which in the Kikuyu language means "Valley") Catholic Parish is a new parish adjoining Our Lady of Visitation Parish in the Eastlands Deanery of Nairobi. The parish has three centers. One of the centers is St. Jude Outstation (subparish) which is located in the very poor, industrial area "slum" section of Mukuru Ruben that has been described by one social worker as follows:

> The Mukuru slums constitute a system of slum settlements strung along the banks of the Ngong River, a murky outlet for toxic chemicals, trash, and human waste which washes its debris into the muddy paths of the villages whenever it rains. The river services the many industries which have grown up along its banks. Desperately poor and landless people come to the city in search of jobs and a better life. Having little or no money, they are forced to live as "squatters" in incredibly dense slums where houses consist of one-room shacks, dirt floors, and often leaky roofs. The average number of people living in one house is seven. The living conditions of the people and what they endure in their daily lives as they struggle to survive is horrible. There is, of course, no electricity or running water. Sanitation facilities consist of a few outdoor pit toilets for thousands of people who have to pay to use them. AIDS, prostitution, alcoholism, and violence are simple facts of life here. And there is often no work.

This center has nine SCCs including St. John SCC, St. Jacinta SCC, and St. Francis SCC. From 4:15 p.m. to 6:15 p.m on Tuesday, 11 June 1996, Archbishop Raphael Ndingi, Mrs. Rose Musimba, and Father Joe Healey participated in a joint prayer meeting and gathering in Swahili of the different SCC leaders which took place in a small dilapidated one-room structure on the local school compound. In individually introducing themselves, the Christians mentioned their ministries, such as Animator of Peace and Animator of Justice and Peace.

The Bible passage was the section on "The Beatitudes" from Mat-

thew 5:1–12. The prayer leader asked the SCC members to choose
and reflect on one particular beatitude that touched their daily lives.
The Bible reflections were very good, especially those of two women
on reconciliation and mercy. The Prayers of the Faithful, which included petitions in Kikuyu and Kamba, two local Kenyan languages,
were very expressive. Intercessory prayers are a very good indicator
of the spirituality and felt needs of the local African people.

After the prayer and Bible reflection we had a one-hour walking
tour of this slum area, learning firsthand the reality of a very poor
section of urban Nairobi. The people are very vulnerable to:

• The weather: rain makes the muddy streets and footpaths a
quagmire and the open sewers a serious health risk. One priest who
regularly visits the area described the scene during the rainy season
in this way:

> We began to leapfrog over ditches of flowing grayish sludge. Watch
> out! Be sure your head ducks under the clothesline right on the
> other side. And "Sorry Mama" for brushing against your clothes.
> Many times we had to break out of our ten abreast formation to
> tiptoe single file over rocks strategically placed in the middle of the
> greenish sloughs which were partly filled with garbage.

• The local authorities: the people could be evicted from their
homes at any time. Presently Kenya is in the throes of a land crisis
with land grabbing and dubious land allocations with many injustices occurring. The poor suffer the most. Often their only recourse
is the Christian churches.

• Sickness and disease: medicine is expensive and AIDS is on the
increase.

The SCCs reflect the changing sociological patterns of African
family life. Most of the SCC members are women—75 percent, according to a recent survey. An increasing number are single mothers.
Research in the SCCs in the slums in Mukuru Ruben and Lunga
Lunga and the river area of Holy Trinity Parish, Buruburu I, indi-
cates that the SCC members and even some of the SCC leaders in
the poorest areas of Nairobi are increasingly single mothers. This
corroborates some general sociological findings on the changing
family in Mukuru Ruben and Lunga Lunga in 1994. A sample taken

of 277 families included 153 single mothers, 81 married couples, and 43 widowed people.

Throughout our visit there was a spirit of spontaneity and joy. Other visitors have remarked on the liveliness, spontaneity, and joy of the liturgies in Mukuru Ruben. Here is one eyewitness account:

> Here we have found the true spirit of community worship. There are many reasons that liturgy in the slums are celebrations and feel like them. There are no diversions such as movies, TV, or other forms of entertainment. People know one another beyond names. When people come together in the liturgical community they are already bonded in real and deep ways. When they hear the Good News they believe it and celebrate. There is joy in this community. Every Sunday they celebrate the presence of God in a special way. Each Sunday one SCC is responsible for the liturgy and the group's banner is proudly displayed. The SCC members are the hosts and hostesses of the day and here in Africa this responsibility is taken seriously. The Sunday Eucharist is a social and spiritual event which brings forth the joy of the people. It is often expressed through both adults and children dancing, singing, and clapping. The celebration includes a lively Exchange of Peace that involves the whole community.

It took us one and a quarter hours (normally a half-hour trip) to drive from Mukuru Ruben back to the Maryknoll Society House in a steady rain during the evening rush hour. Even this had a message for us: the transportation hardships of poor people in our African cities. Overall we realized that such visits are a great support and encouragement to Christians living in the urban slums. They appreciate that other people care. This shows the importance of more exchange visits between SCC members in different parts of the city.

Implications and Challenges

1. First, there is the challenge of the long, slow, and winding process of moving from a Christian prayer group or a small group of any kind to a genuine and authentic SCC. Archbishop Ndingi remarked that "SCCs are still young," having been started in 1973, 1976, and as late as 1986 in certain dioceses in Eastern Africa. Yet with the present dose of piety and spiritual devotion among many

African Christians, moving to SCCs with a real spirit of inculturation, service, and transformation of society is very difficult. John
Waliggo criticizes the SCCs for not being involved enough in justice
and peace issues in Uganda, for example, during the recent democratization process.

2. An important feature of the SCC prayer and Bible reflection
is to start with life and to share life. Archbishop Ndingi posed:
"Why don't our Sunday liturgies [or perhaps the homily/sermon]
start with the important events in our lives during the past week?"
Take the example of Bariadi Parish in Shinyanga Diocese, Tanzania,
which is composed of twenty-four SCCs in a small town (district)
setting. The parish priest participates in the weekday lives and activities of the SCCs so he has a very good "feel" of the pulse of the
daily lives of the Christians. On Sunday when the SCC members
gather for the Sunday parish Eucharist it is as "a union of SCCs."
In his homily the priest reflects back to, and with the people, the
SCC experiences of the previous week in light of the Sunday Scripture readings. He does not have to invent his own sermon. He starts
with the life and experiences of the people, especially in the SCCs.

3. In many ways the African family is in crisis, especially in urban
areas such as Nairobi. In light of our experiences in Mukuru Ruben
maybe "Church as Neighborhood" fits the African context better
than "Church as Family" as Aylward Shorter has pointed out. This
includes not only the geographical location but a real sense of people
sharing as neighbors and helping each other in the biblical sense of
"neighbor."

4. The Christian churches have to meet the African people and
African families "where they are at." This means adapting to the
fast-changing urban realities in Africa. One phenomenon in urban
Eastern Africa is the increasing number of single mothers. Already
parishes in Nakuru and Nairobi have started clubs or groups of
single mothers. The SCCs need to be more sensitive to the difficult
lives and struggles of these single mothers and support their groups
and discussions.

Yet we noticed that while these single mothers are very active
in discussing their local problems and frustrations in their various
single mother clubs, they do not bring these social and economic

problems to their SCC meetings. They look on their SCCs as prayer groups with pious devotions as a kind of spiritual "escape" from their daily problems. The SCCs serve as a spiritual buffer or fortress in a survival situation and are an important source of long-range spiritual hope.

II. Sociology of the Changing African Family

The African family—especially the large or "so-called" extended family—is under strong pressure today. One threat is the separation of family members and even of spouses through migrant labor. This puts a strain on marriages and is a major factor in desertion and divorce. Due to the dispersal of family members, families operate in a truncated manner in both urban and rural areas. Family roles are amalgamated or improvised.

Another threat is posed by the generation gap. This is the physical and psychological distance between parents and children, especially those receiving secondary or tertiary education. The generation gap affects family life and especially marriage. Young people aspire to choose their partners freely, but parents still control the institution of marriage through bridewealth and traditional rituals. Young people tend to enter casual and trial unions, keeping their options open. This leads to considerable moral disorientation, sexual promiscuity, and the prevalence of single-parent households, especially in towns. Traditional authoritarianism and sexism in families are less and less tolerated by the youth, who constitute more than half the population and who demand to be given responsibility.

Single-parent households also result from wives who separate from their irresponsible husbands because of the men's drinking, anger resulting in wife-beating, and financial mismanagement. Other single women choose to have children outside of marriage and prefer to live alone without the "burden" of a husband.

Urbanization affects the African family by making family hospitality and sharing difficult. It also introduces the money element into family relationships, and this undermines the social and religious aspects of family life and institutions. See, for example, its effects on bridewealth.

Customary marriages are less stable than formerly, and while divorce is relatively rare among those with a church marriage, the customary marriages of Christians are notoriously unstable. Polygamy, in its classic form of simultaneous plural marriage, is declining. It tends to be a form of desertion by the husband, who takes a second wife according to custom, without the formality of a divorce or formal separation.

Familism (nepotism) remains strong in Africa. This is the tendency to support and favor family members at the expense of other social and professional obligations. Family networks remain an important means of securing jobs and improving incomes.

Family values are also threatened by the mass media and especially by the new video culture which favors pornography, violence, and romantic stories. Youth pop culture is also affected by violence and sexual exploitation in entertainment forms, e.g. Gangsta-Rap and the sexually explicit pop music and dances from Zaire (Kwasa-Kwasa and Rumba).

There is no doubt that the family in Africa faces a serious challenge to cope with social change and with the impact of the mass media. It needs the support of small Christian communities and of various parish associations if it is to be renewed.

Another example comes from Dar es Salaam, Tanzania. Infant baptisms took place in Mtoni Parish in Dar es Salaam Archdiocese in July 1996. Of the fourteen children who were registered eleven were children of single parents—ten mothers and one father. These were a mixture of single parents who had broken up with their spouses or women who had given birth outside of marriage/wedlock. The parish priest said this was the first time he had experienced this phenomenon to such a drastic proportion—a phenomenon which is a growing reality, especially in urban Africa.

III. Developing a Theological Method from Below

To achieve meaningful success in any major ecclesial initiative or experiment in our contemporary church, a well thought out theology and methodology are a must. Such a theology should be done with and by the people concerned. It should grow as the communities grow and multiply and meet various contexts and experiences. Social analysis of church and society and the people's aspirations, desires, felt needs, problems, fears, and anxieties provide the sources for such a theology. Any relevant theology today has to take people's cultures and history into serious consideration. Only when all this is carried out can an ecclesial initiative be judged relevant and likely to achieve positive change in people's lives, attitudes, and mentality and thus transform church and society.

Various African theologians have stated that when the bishops in Eastern Africa launched the SCCs in 1973, 1976, and 1979 they underestimated the importance of a guiding theology for the experiment. The initiative came from the bishops, and it was implemented as a policy by the parish clergy and their pastoral teams. African theologians were not given a clear role. The Christians at the grass roots became recipients. This top-to-bottom methodology could not enable the SCCs to achieve all that the bishops enthusiastically expected of them.

There are many ways of being and living community in Africa. The last hundred years of evangelization have formed different types of Christian communities in Africa, depending on the missionary style, formation, mentality, and diversity of the evangelizers. When the SCCs were introduced, it was not possible nor desirable to conceive them in a uniform manner. What some bishops saw as a novelty in the SCCs was already an accepted practice in other local churches.

The models of SCCs differed. Some wanted to recreate the original communities described in Acts of the Apostles, chapters 2 and 4. Some had in mind the African traditional communities based on "so-called" extended families. Some were animated by the model of the Mystical Body of Christ as described in I Corinthians, chapter 12. Others wanted them to be entirely new creations demanded by the pastoral strategies of the times. These various models were not studied in depth nor related to each other. An initiative which should have been presented as coming directly from the way the African people live community was thus missed. SCCs necessitated new guidelines, new formation in setting them up, and a certain discontinuity from the way that the African Church was normally growing. It was this unnecessary emphasis on the "newness" of the

SCCs which has hindered their widespread growth and their being a true source of inculturation.

In practice the SCCs are taken as simply an addition to the old way of being church. The institutional model of church under hierarchical, clerical, and often paternalistic control is still the most dominant. The church is still power- and authority-centered. Old attitudes, styles of leadership, and structures dominate. Some promoters of SCCs try to point out the conflict between the old and the new way of being church. Often they identify the clergy and catechists as the major obstacles to SCCs. Whoever does not promote SCCs is regarded as "conservative" and whoever does is seen as "progressive." The tension here, however, is more complex. The problem goes back to the very beginning of the initiative and the failure to place it fully under the people at the grass roots.

The aims of the SCCs were not clearly and powerfully articulated from the very beginning. This may have been for reasons of fear and "prudence." SCCs were initiated because the participation of the laity in the church and evangelization was weak. The institutional model of church had "suffocated" the community aspect and dimension. However given Africa's most oppressive problems of poverty, disease, suppression of human rights, wars and conflicts, dictatorships and exploitation, it is shocking to find that the SCCs did not take these issues as fundamental in their vision and activities. SCCs have not been in the forefront for the struggle for justice and peace, human rights and democratization. The absence of these issues on their agenda is one of the main reasons for the absence of men, youth, and professionals in SCCs.

The contemporary theologies that can redeem this experiment of SCCs are:

• A theology of *liberation* from all that enslaves Africa and Africans, both in church and society.

• A theology of *inculturation* which can empower African Christians to feel fully at home in the church and to be the judges of the fruitful interaction between the gospel and cultures.

• A theology of *communion*, not only of Catholics but of the entire People of God, as it was and still is in the authentically African communities. SCCs must not only be ecumenical but must relate perfectly with all people without any discrimination.

• A *contextual* theology which pays attention to the differences in the needs and aspirations of the rural and the urban, the educated and the illiterate, the old and the young.

• A *narrative* theology which interprets the wide range of narrative and oral forms of SCCs—proverbs, sayings, riddles, stories, myths, plays, and songs—in their historical, cultural, and religious contexts.

It is such theologies that can and should develop from below in order to answer effectively the needs of the times. It is these theologies than can help to "open up" the church to democratization and empower the SCCs to become the pillars for the kingdom values of justice and peace, human dignity and total liberation. We need a diversity of models to meet the desired goals. We need to relate these models in such a way that unity in diversity becomes the hope and approach for the liberation and transformation of church and society in Africa.

It is not just the academic theologians from the top down who will develop this new theology but also ordinary SCC members from the bottom up. This is part of what Robert Schreiter, of the Catholic Theological Union (Chicago), calls "the local community as theologian."

As many theologians ask, Has our theology been too much "theology from above," and do the small Christian communities offer hope of building a theology from the grass-roots level, from the lives of ordinary people, a theology from below? Part of the answer may come in the SCCs being "the local community as theologian." A new way of being church correlates with a new way of doing theology. This is related to constructing local theologies and the development of a people's theology, a popular theology. Bible sharing and the reflections of SCC members can be examples of the local community as theologian. Sometimes the animator or advisor relates the content and the specific reflection process to the wider traditions of the world Church. Timira describes how this could work:

Ultimately the *pastoral hermeneutic circle* could help us in enhancing the growth of SCCs through its fivefold process of: insertion, analysis, reflection, pastoral planning, and praxis. Thus starting with current issues or burning questions, the SCC venture will no doubt proceed beyond the pastoral model to one of social-political conscientization and change in the light of the gospel and church teaching.

One of the African contributions to the world Church is "the local African Christian community theologizing." Local gatherings of SCCs reflecting on their daily lives in light of the gospel (and reflecting on the gospel in the light of their daily lives) can be a real theological locus or theological moment. There are an increasing number of case studies and examples of theology developing in an African context as an African narrative theology of inculturation and liberation. This is an example of Schreiter's contextual model of a local theology.

It is important to point out that the church is not simply visible, nor solely human. It is and remains a mystery. As such it cannot be reduced to any one image or model, however useful. All models (see the examples in Avery Dulles' classic book *Models of Church*) ought to go together in an inclusive manner. New models ought to continue to be found as inculturation grows and people's social context becomes modified. In any local church at any one moment there is a need to emphasize all relevant models. There is no one ecclesiology but several ecclesiologies. Different circumstances, occasions, celebrations and sufferings in every locality necessitates emphasizing the model of church that best fits the occasion. In schools the church is foremost a *herald church,* announcing the Good News to all. In a refugee camp the church must be a truly *serving* or *servant church.* In time of war the church must be a truly *reconciling church.*

IV. Church as Family as a New Ecclesiological Model or Image

The main theological theme or model or image of the 1994 African Synod was *Church as Family* or *Church as Family of God.* In the development of ecclesiology, Church as Family is a new theological category which can deepen the present understanding of "church." This theme developed from, and built on, the image of the People of God of the Second Vatican Council. The synod portrayed this dominant model of church as a family through such terms as Church as Brotherhood, Church as the Family of God, and Church-Family. The vision of the church as God's family has a natural appeal to African people. This ecclesiology of Church as Family emphasizes the warmth of love among widely extended relationships and an authority that finds its proper context in service. No. 63 of *Ecclesia in Africa (The Church in Africa)*, Pope John Paul II's Apostolic Exhortation on the African Synod (14 September 1995) on "The Church as God's Family" states:

> Not only did the Synod speak of inculturation, but it also made use of it, taking the Church as God's Family as its guiding idea for the evangelization of Africa. The Synod Fathers acknowledged it as an expression of the Church's nature particularly appropriate for Africa. For this image emphasizes care for others, solidarity, warmth in human relationships, acceptance, dialogue and trust.

The bishops emphasized the great value in the church's social teaching that every person belongs to the same family of God. John Mary Waliggo states:

> The bishops could have chosen the Vatican II concept of church as *Communion* or as *People of God*. They purposely chose Church as Family; they wanted to use the African family as the model for being and living church. The family model includes everyone, baptized and non-baptized, involving every member. It serves well the emphasis on Small Christian Communities.

The expression Church as Family appeared fifteen times in the *Final Message* of the 1994 African Synod and is described as follows:

1. "Has its origin in the Blessed Trinity at the depths of which the Holy Spirit is the bond of communion" (No. 20).
2. "Manifests to the world the Spirit which the Son sent from the Father so that there should be communion among all" (No. 24).
3. "Christ has come to restore the world to unity, a single hu-

man family in the image of the trinitarian family. We are the family of God: this is the good news" (No. 25).
4. "Is a church of communion" (No. 57).

In the synod documentation the Church as Family of God is also described as follows:

> The African sense of family solidarity affords a valuable base on which to build an ecclesiology of the church as the "Family of God" on earth. In this ecclesiology, Living Christian Communities [SCCs] form cells within which love of God is inseparable from love of neighbor, and in which the tendencies to disunity—egoism, tribalism, etc.—are discerned and overcome.

Listen to the African Synod's specific words to the Christian family in No. 27 of the *Final Message:*

> The vitality of the Church as Family, which the synod wishes to highlight, can only be effective insofar as all our Christian families become authentic domestic churches. . . . The extended African family is the sacred place where all the riches of our tradition converge. It is therefore the task of you Christian families to bring to the heart of this extended family a witness which transforms from the inside our vision of the world.

Waliggo points out the danger of using the image of family uncritically to describe the reality of the church in Africa. He cautions that the Family of God should not be a patriarchical structure in which bishops, priests, and religious are the parents and the laity are children. The Family of God in Africa has to be redesigned in order to give the laity—and especially lay women—their rightful responsibility. He explains:

> The theology of Church as Family is a two-edged sword. It can be profitably used but may also lead to benign paternalism. Before it is applied the image of the family must be fully liberated. We should not once again end up with a pyramid structure of the church but rather a circular one of communion.

In No. 28 of the *Final Message* the section on "The Church as Family and Small Christian Communities" states:

The Church, the Family of God, implies the creation of small communities at the human level, living or Christian base communities. In such communities, which are cells of the Church as Family, one is formed to live concretely and authentically the experience of fraternity. In them the spirit of disinterested service, solidarity and common goals reigns. Each is moved to construct the Family of God, a family entirely open to the world from which absolutely nobody is excluded. It is such communities that will provide the best means to fight against ethnocentrism within the church itself and, more widely, within our nations. These individual Churches as Families have the task of working to transform society.

The core of this text appeared in Propositio 9 and finally in *Ecclesia in Africa (The Church in Africa)* in No. 89 under "Living (or Vital) Christian Communities"

Right from the beginning, the Synod Fathers recognized that the Church as Family cannot reach her full potential as Church unless she is divided into communities small enough to foster close human relationships. The Assembly described the characteristics of such communities as follows: primarily they should be places engaged in evangelizing themselves, so that subsequently they can bring the Good News to others; they should moreover be communities which pray and listen to God's Word, encourage the members themselves to take on responsibility, learn to live an ecclesial life, and reflect on different human problems in the light of the gospel. Above all, these communities are to be committed to living Christ's love for everybody, a love which transcends the limits of natural solidarity of clans, tribes, or other interest groups.

No. 56 of the *Final Message* of the 1994 African Synod offered the following words to African theologians:

Your mission is a great and noble one in the service of inculturation which is the important work site for the development of African theology. You have already begun to propose an African reading of the mystery of Christ. The concepts of Church as Family, Church as Brotherhood are the fruits of your work in contact with the Christian experience of the People of God in Africa.

Based on Propositio 8 the pope states in No. 63, under "The

Church As God's Family," "It is earnestly to be hoped that theologians in Africa will work out the theology of the Church as Family with all the riches contained in this concept, showing its complementarity with other images of the Church." James Corboy emphasizes:

> The work of the theologians must be based, like all theology, on the experiences of the people. To play a primary part in developing a theology of Church as Family in Africa, I think one would have to have an experience of living in an African family and participating in a Small Christian Community, or to have been intimately associated with them.

This preferred model of Church as Family of God in the African Synod should start with experience and the local context. Also it is not exclusive, but inclusive of all other models. It encourages theological, ecclesiological, and pastoral pluralism within the African Church. Within it all other models must be stressed.

V. Constructing an Ecclesiology of Church as Family and Small Christian Communities

Let us start with the experience of African people. In developing an ecclesiology of Church as Family it is important to understand the unique qualities of the African family—quite different from the Western notion of family (for example, the nuclear family). Some African theologians do not like the term "extended family," saying that "extended family" is really a Western term used as a way of interpreting the traditional African family. But it is clear that the African family is "large."

Two important distinctions have to be made in describing the African family. First, Waliggo states: "The African family incorporates, in a unique manner, all the living members, however scattered, the living dead (to use John Mbiti's expression) and the generations yet unborn." The dead members can be further distinguished between the ancestors of long ago and the recently deceased. Second, the living members of an African family comprise three contemporary generations who share their earthly existence together—the grandparents, the parents, and the children, including aunts, uncles, and cousins.

The traditional African family is in crisis, especially in urban areas such as Nairobi, Dar es Salaam, and Lusaka. Sociological realities are busy breaking down irreversibly the whole family ethos in African society, especially due to the economic difficulties that people are facing and the influence of secularism. There is abundant sociological evidence of a correlation between urbanization and secularism, and the modern media are a notable element in the spread of an urban mentality. There are also numerous signs that secularism is growing in the African city. African family institutions are under threat from modern social processes. The African family today is living in religious, political, economic, cultural, social, and environmental *pluralism*. The real challenge is: How are we to make of this changing reality of the African family a credible model for constructing the church in Africa?

Now let us look at the reality of SCCs. Today on the practical, grass-roots level in Eastern Africa most of the SCCs are a "Pastoral Model" that develops within the parish structures. The common rural model is a communion of members of large families in the same neighborhood or geographical area. The common urban model usually groups people who live near each other in a row of houses or an apartment house or a workers' housing project. Yet new forms of Christian community are emerging in cities such as Nairobi and Lusaka which are not small communities in the strict sense but are networks or unions of Christians living in the same section or district. There are a growing number of urban SCCs based on occupation or common interests, such as youth, workers, nurses, and charismatic prayer groups. NOTE: Up until now Eastern Africa has relatively few "marginal" or "critical" SCCs which exist outside of the formal structures and teachings of the Catholic Church. Yet these types of SCCs are growing rapidly in other parts of the world.

The present SCCs reflect these changing sociological patterns of African family life as described above in the recent research on SCCs in Nairobi. As another example, government statistics in Zambia show increasing figures for categories such as no-parent families; parentless children; child households; and households headed by females under fourteen years old. This is mainly due to parents dying of AIDS. This has many implications for the changing composition and praxis of SCCs.

Different theologies help to evolve a new ecclesiology:

1. *Trinitarian Communion Ecclesiology*

Church as Family of God is challenged to fit the egalitarian model needed for a theology of Church as Family with parallels to trinitarian theology. This new family is rooted, not in biological kinship, but in the Trinity. The head of this family is God. Human families and all types of church communities are invited to take the Trinity as their model. The Church as Family of God is founded on the trinitarian unity and solidarity of the three divine persons. It is this unity which continues to challenge the church to promote *koinonia* among all God's people.

The African family can also be described as "Africa's domestic church" and "the icon of the Trinity on earth." It is the most effective means for humanizing and personalizing society.

Every Christian community, every SCC, in some way reflects the trinitarian communion, which is its source, and ecclesial communion, which is its sign. There is an African saying: "If God lives as a community, we must do the same." SCC members are called to a life of sharing modeled on the Trinity, as described by Bishop Christopher Mwoleka:

> I think we have difficulties in understanding the Holy Trinity because we approach the mystery from the wrong side. The intellectual side is not the best side to start with. The right approach to the mystery is to imitate the life of the Trinity, which is a life of sharing. . . . I am dedicated to the ideal of *Ujamaa* [Swahili for "Familyhood"] because it invites all people, in a down-to-earth, practical way, to imitate the life of the Trinity, which is a life of sharing.

2. *Communion Ecclesiology*

Already back in 1973 the AMECEA Study Conference in Nairobi stated that to achieve a truly African local church

We have to insist on building church life and work on Christian base Communities in both rural and urban areas. Church life must be based on the communities in which everyday life and work take place: those basic and manageable social groups whose members can experience real interpersonal relationships and feel a sense of communal belonging, both in living and working.

Eastern Africa has stressed a theology of incarnation and communion ecclesiology. Archbishop Raphael Ndingi Mwana'a Nzeki states: "In East Africa a new approach to ecclesiology is evolving. It is based on the concept of the church as a communion of communities, a two-way sharing between communities." This *communion of communities* focus is closely related to the African values of fraternity and sharing. This new approach contrasts the old model of church on the local level ("Service Station or Pipe Line Theory Model") with the new model ("Small Christian Community Model of Church as a New Way of Being Church"). This new SCC-centered ecclesiology is contrasted with the traditional parish-centered ecclesiology. This Small Christian Community Model of Church is based on the church as communion (*koinonia*). Starting from the bottom up:

- A SCC is a communion of families.
- An outstation or subparish is a communion of SCCs.
- A parish is a communion of outstations or subparishes
- The diocese is a communion of parishes.

In light of recent experiences in urban areas of Eastern Africa, especially among the urban poor, the "Theology of Church as Neighborhood" may fit the African context better. SCCs are increasingly composed of a wide variety of Christians who gather together in the same neighborhood. Participation of both the father and mother of the same family/household is rare. Very few young people participate unless they have their own Youth SCCs. Aylward Shorter states:

> SCCs are related to the traditional and highly relevant African concept of neighborhood. Many institutions and rituals occur at neighborhood level, e.g., reconciliation rites, redressive rituals, neighborhood courts and assemblies, etc. SCCs are sometimes viewed as a

"surrogate family," or as "groups of families." Some writers have even argued for kinship-based SCCs, and in some cases this is the actual reality. The practical problem is: How to transcend the family and use it as a model for wider ecclesial reconstruction.

Some of these SCCs focus more on "neighborhood" than on church, that is, their activities and energy come more from the ties to their local community and geographical location than their ties to the Catholic Church structures. The emphasis is on immersion into the daily life of the local community. This style of SCC has far-reaching implications for a more inclusive and ecumenical way of being church. Ecumenism is not an appendix to the nature of the church, but central.

3. Ancestral Ecclesiology

The Church as Family of God can be promoted through a rich Christology of "Christ as Ancestor." In the corresponding ancestral ecclesiology, God is the ultimate ancestor and source of all being. One research study shows that among the 232 African names and descriptions of Jesus Christ the most common are names connected to Jesus as "Ancestor," as "Brother," and as "Intercessor-Mediator." Various African theologians such as Benezet Bujo, Francois Kabasele, Emmanuel Milingo, Charles Nyamiti, John Pobee, and Anselme Sanon have written about ancestral Christology, ancestral kinship, and Christ's brother-ancestorship. Jesus is the "Ancestor of Christians," "Ancestor Par Excellence," "Ancestor Who Is the Source of Life," "Divine Ancestor," "First Ancestor," "Founder of the Great Family," "Great Ancestor," "Great Ancestral Spirit," "Great and Greatest Ancestor," "Highest Model of Ancestorship," "Holy Ancestral Spirit," "Proto-Ancestor," "Supreme Universal Ancestral Spirit" and "Unique Ancestor."

Ancestral ecclesiology incorporates all members, the living and the living dead together. Ancestors are integral to the living family community. SCC members feel themselves to be part of the family of Jesus. He is the "Eldest Brother." In fact, the image of the spiritual family of Jesus strongly appeals to SCCs in Africa. "For whoever does the will of my Father in heaven is my brother and sister and mother" (Matt. 12:50). It is important to continue to bring this theology's message to the everyday experiences of SCCs for their enrichment and empowerment.

4. *Liberation and Transformation Ecclesiology*

What can positively influence the current disintegration of the African family, especially in urban areas, and adequately empower people and SCCs to be active in the social transformation of church and society is the ecclesiology of liberation. The African family experiences poverty, injustices, conflicts, the scourge of AIDS, the oppression of women, and the violation of the rights of the child. The combined action of SCCs in social involvement can help to liberate and transform the African family, support the women's movement to achieve basic equality, and give sure hope to those who feel helpless in oppressive situations.

The long journey of SCCs in Eastern Africa continues with great hope for church and society. The experiences of these communities form a basis for the development of relevant bottom-up Christologies and ecclesiologies. There is no doubt that SCCs are a great asset in building up the Church as Family of God and a real center for the inculturation of the Christian faith in Africa.

Select Bibliography

1994 Special Assembly for Africa of the Synod of Bishops. *Final Message* and *64 Propositions*. Vatican City, 1994.

Africa Faith and Justice Network. *The African Synod: Documents, Reflections, Perspectives*. Maryknoll, N.Y.: Orbis Books, 1996.

Background Papers and Final Statement of the International Consultation on Basic Christian Communities. Notre Dame, Ind.: Institute for Pastoral and Social Ministry, University of Notre Dame, 1991.

"Church as Family of God." *Lineamenta* for the 1997 SECAM Plenary Assembly. Accra: unpublished paper, 1995. 41 pp.

Corboy, James. "Church as Communio and Family of God." *SEDOS Bulletin* 96 (15 May 1996): 156–159.

Healey, Joseph. "Twelve Case Studies of Small Christian Communities (SCCs) in Eastern Africa," in Agatha Radoli, ed., *How Local is the Local Church: Small Christian Communities and Church in Eastern Africa*. Eldoret: *Spearhead* No. 126–28, 1993: 96–99.

Healey, Joseph and Donald Sybertz. *Towards an African Narrative Theology*. Nairobi: Paulines Publications Africa, 1996, and Maryknoll, N.Y.: Orbis Books, 1997. See especially the "Foreword" by Raphael Ndingi Mwana'a Nzeki and chapter 3 on "Church as the Extended Family of God."

John Paul II. Post Synodal Apostolic Exhortation *The Church in Africa*. Nairobi: Paulines Publications Africa, 1995.

Mwoleka, Christopher, and Joseph Healey, eds. *Ujamaa and Christian Communities*. Eldoret: *Spearhead* No. 45, 1976.

Ndingi, Raphael. "Basic Communities: The African Experience," in *A New Missionary Era*. Maryknoll, N.Y.: Orbis Books, 1982.

Shorter, Aylward. *The African Synod*. Nairobi: St. Paul Publications—Africa, 1993.

——. *The Church in the African City*. Maryknoll, N.Y.: Orbis Books, 1991.

——. "The Family as a Model for Social Reconstruction in Africa." Nairobi: forthcoming in *Tangaza Occasional Papers*, 1997. 13 pp.

"Small Christian Communities in the Light of the African Synod." *AMECEA Documentation Service*, 453 (1 April, 1996). See especially Joseph Healey, "Implementing the Synod Seminar for Members of SCCs—Tanzania" (1–2) and "Important Dates and Quotations in the History and Development of SCCs in Africa, Especially in the AMECEA Countries" (7–8). Rita Ishengoma, "A Clay Cooking Pot, Image of a Caring Community" (3).

Waliggo, John Mary. "The African Clan as the True Model of the African Church," in J. N. K. Mugambi and Laurenti Magesa, eds., *The Church in African Christianity: Innovative Essays in Ecclesiology*. Nairobi: Initiatives Publishers, 1990.

——. "The Church as Family of God and Small Christian Communities." *AMECEA Documentation Service*, No. 429 (1 December, 1994): 1.

——. "Making a Church That is Truly African," in J. M. Waliggo, et al., *Inculturation: Its Meaning and Urgency*. Nairobi: St. Paul Publications—Africa, 1986: 30.

——. "Uganda Episcopal Conference Programme of Implementing the African Synod: The Church as Family Constructed on Justice and Peace." Kampala: unpublished paper, 1996. 13 pp.

THE CONSULTATION STATEMENT
TO THE WIDER CHURCH

Dear friends, greetings! We came from many places in the world and traveled far to talk together about being followers of Jesus in small communities in many places. We were gladdened and encouraged to hear of and learn about the many, many other groups. We join with all of them and with you in prayer and hope in Christ as we are, all together, building the Church.

People of the Notre Dame Gathering
October 24, 1996
Notre Dame, Indiana

I. Introduction

Nature and Purpose of Gathering

We gathered in theological consultation to reflect specifically on the theology emerging within small Christian communities.[1] The Consultation was intended to be inclusive of community experience throughout the world. To that end participants were present from all continents except Europe.

The Consultation occurred in the context of the teachings of Vatican II, especially *Lumen Gentium*, as "a holy People of God" who "spread abroad a living witness to God, especially by a life of faith and love and by offering to God a sacrifice of praise. . . . " The Consultation also occurred against the background of prior reflections on small Christian communities, including the United States experience of small Christian communities (1990, Notre Dame,

---

[1] The Consultation has elected to use the term "small Christian community" to include Christian base communities, intentional eucharistic communities, and small Christian communities.

Ind.) and the international experience of small Christian communities (1991, Notre Dame, Ind.). The present gathering was intended
to reflect specifically on the Christology and the ecclesiology that
may be emerging within and identified from the experience of those
in small Christian communities.

II. Methodology

The methodology for the Consultation was that of the communities themselves. In narrative, participants shared the concrete of
lives being lived in small Christian communities. The Consultation
listened to the specifics of diverse experiences of small Christian
community throughout the world and spent three days in dialogue
with these experiences. Then, in a fourth day, began the narrower
process of discerning the Christology and ecclesiology manifest in
the disclosed experiences. This document is not the end but the con-
tinuation of that process of discernment.

III. Practices of the Communities

The process yielded three questions of fruitful inquiry. Why do
these communities gather? What do they do when they gather?
What is the impact of the gathering on the members and the ecclesial and civil world?

Why do communities gather?

We found small Christian communities gather for very basic, fundamental reasons. As basic as a simple NEED felt for gathering. A
sense surfaced that relationship in gathering is a basic human need.
It makes no difference whether in Africa, South America, Latin
America, Australia, Hong Kong, North America, or India. We have,
in common, experienced the universal human need for the gathering. Additionally, proximate causes for gathering may vary within
specific political, economic, or social contexts. In Africa, causes for
small Christian communities include pastoral reasons; in Latin and
South America and India the causes may include matters of survival,
solidarity, and empowerment; in North America, Australia, or Hong

Kong the cause may include matters of relationship, growth, support. But while the experiences come from diverse circumstances, the need for and presence of Christian community attaches to all human circumstances—impoverished or affluent, oppressed or powerful. The human heart seeks community—it is the expression of human need for GOD.

What do communities do when they gather?

The communities gather to remember in story their whole Christian tradition. Principally by returning to Sacred Scripture, communities seek not just who Jesus was, or who some say he was, but what Jesus did in his life and what he disclosed of the reign of God. In entering the stories of Jesus' active life, communities discover the intimate, relational, and human Jesus—a person concrete, available within their own human experience. In so doing, they also discover that the humanity of Jesus discloses the mystery of his divinity. The communities have discovered that this dialogue with their tradition now motivates and empowers those who have gathered to behave in their own circumstances as they perceived the meaning of Jesus' own behavior. And thus they become the healer, the ancestor, the neighbor, the suffering servant, the liberator/transformer they understood Jesus to be. In Latin America, communities thus gathered are understood as participating in and becoming the project of God.

In the gathered relationships, members discover the divine within us, the mystery of the divine in human life. They experience the Incarnation in a concrete manner. Communities realize a sense of the Trinitarian God, creator, redeemer, life-giving spirit in communion with each other as members grasp the reality of their own interdependent relationships.

In narrative, between Sacred Scripture and the community, members experience tensions between what they are becoming and what are the current social, political, and economic realities of their lives. Indeed, in the narrative, community members bring not just personal circumstances but broader regional, national, and global social and political realities. In their narratives a mutually critical dialogue between our sacred stories and our experienced culture is carried out. Gospel stories challenged by specific individual lives yield answers which in turn challenge lives and times. It is a dialogue between God and God's people.

What is the impact of small Christian communities on their members, the civil and ecclesial worlds?

1. Impact on members. We found that in all small Christian communities, members are always in the process of being gathered in to be sent out. The impact is fuller sharing in the mission of Jesus. The community and its members are impelled outward in mission to live:

in solidarity with the poor;
with compassion for all in need;
with hospitality for the stranger.

In this sending the communities realize a deeper meaning of Eucharist—Eucharist which is not only celebrated as memory but lived as an ongoing process of blessing, breaking and sharing our very lives for the sake of *all* God's entire creation. In their small Christian communities, members have *experienced,* through their brothers and sisters, that the reign of God truly belongs to all—regardless of age, race, sex, faith, nationality, or physical condition, each must reach out in communion to all. It is not enough simply to be inclusive; the communities have realized that, like their brother Jesus, they must be invitational as well. In doing this, the community becomes a sacrament of presence to all. In truth it becomes church—an embryonic church in which the total church is present. The community over time enkindles and treasures memories that are radically lived out in a simple way of life—but a dangerous way because it constantly challenges the reality around us by our gospel roots.

The small Christian community has become the locus for formation and conversion of the individual. As members reflect on Scriptures, in conversation with social and political realities, members become aware of lies and illusions, oppression and injustices within dominant secular cultures. We realize that our own actions may be contributing to the structures which breed injustice, poverty, alienation.

But in small Christian communities the member also begins to appreciate that society can truly be different from that which the dominant culture would tell us. We see this possibility because we realize we each can take the risk of giving birth to this new reality. We can bring into existence a society that includes respect for diversity, sharing resources, welcoming presence—humankind as the family of God, as Jesus promised and exemplified. This community, therefore, enables its members to draw and honor the memory of Jesus with the hope, ever being actualized in individual lives, of the coming of the reign of God.

The participants listened to statements from various base Christian communities of Brazil that concretely exemplified the universal impact of small Christian community on individuals:

> "Joy has become part of our lives because of our experience of God."
>
> "The gospel is applied to our lives and to the suffering of the people."
>
> "We feel more human and happier."
>
> "We feel more free to speak up."
>
> "We have learned; we follow the way."
>
> "We show love; we have seen Jesus in our sisters and brothers."
>
> "We are more interested in our families and neighbors."
>
> "We have gathered together around the Word of God."
>
> "We have become more patient with the family and other people."
>
> "We have learned forgiveness, tolerance, and acceptance of differences."
>
> "We have learned to be grateful to God."

2. *Impact on the Ecclesial World.* Small Christian community has become a means for formation of laity within Catholic tradition. In some regions, notably East Africa, it has also become a pastoral vehicle of the church. The practical but rich experience of small Christian community throughout the world is a model of church available for favorable consideration by bishops in their national synods. It is an experience of church which is as universal as the human family but as diverse as the unique circumstances of each member of that family. The ongoing experience of small Christian commu-

nity is a hopeful sign for the church of collegiality, collaboration, equality, and shared gifts in church. Small Christian community has both been nurtured by and in turn has nurtured a servant leadership. The communities and their leadership have functioned as prophets within the church.

3. *Impact on Civil World.* Formed in their small Christian communities, individually and collectively members have taken gospel values to their families, neighborhoods, workplaces. Both to the poor, in solidarity, and to the wealthy and powerful, in challenge, communities have sent members. There are stories of change. But the poor remain; the oppressive structures stand. It is the faith and hope of small Christian communities that the Spirit of God is using their members to bring the peace and justice of Christ finally to the world.

IV. Biblical Image for the Communities

The Consultation recognized an applicable biblical image for small Christian communities in Luke 13:13–35, the Emmaus story. Members experience the journey on the road to Emmaus in which, along with Cleopas and his companion, troubled by the events of their times, their hearts are inflamed and enlightened by the very presence of the Risen Jesus. In gathering, they remember and recognize him in the breaking of the bread—and more concretely, recognize him in and through their own brokenness. They have glimpsed the resurrected Christ, but we realize the reign of God still remains elusive. In the instant of recognition, Jesus vanishes and they experience again the need to return to the gathering, to tell what has happened and experience again the process. The road will not end until there is peace and justice among all; and the road has no resting place. It moves through deserts and gardens. Along its way is the continuing discovery of the divine within the human, within the gathering, within our narratives in dialogue with Scriptures. But from the community, we are always and continually being sent forth again in the mission to everyone in this process of small

Christian community. There is always the ongoing, relived journey to Emmaus.

V. Christology

The Christology evidenced in small Christian community very much proceeds from the humanity of Jesus, as encountered in Scripture and referenced in individual lives. The communities are engaged by not just what Jesus said, but more so by what he did. They instinctively understand that the actions of Jesus illuminate his words. In this process, the communities experience an intimate, relational, humanity of Jesus which opens the revelation of the creating, redeeming, and sustaining God—Father, Son, and Spirit. This is an "ascending" Christology in which the divine is available through encounter with the human—in Jesus and in one another. Jesus thus encountered in small Christian community becomes, *inter alia*, brother, healer, neighbor, agitator, outsider, ancestor, friend, liberator, teacher—images of Jesus drawn from individual circumstances of the diverse communities. In each image, however, is the presence of Christ among his people in the particulars of their lives.

VI. Ecclesiology

In small Christian communities, there is manifest church which is ancient but ever new. It is rooted in the primitive communities of the Acts of the Apostles. The church in community is a global reality, in varying stages of process, impacting everywhere. There is no one style. In South America the ecclesiology includes: Scripture leading to conversion; community as *koinonia;* Eucharist as sacrament and prayer; missionary character, aiming at the reign of God; and apostolic character, connected to tradition. It is church which is a transforming presence in society. In Africa the ecclesiology followed its Christology in the following manner:

Jesus as healer	healing ministry
Jesus as ancestor	family ministry
Jesus as neighbor	communion

| Jesus as suffering servant | servant ministry |
| Jesus as liberator | participation and liberation |

In North America there is no common expressible style, as communities continue to grow and develop and use varying styles. From AustralAsia the Consultation heard ecclesiology which was open, ecumenical, and inclusive. All styles, however, shared common elements of "see, judge, act" strategies. But in all instances, it is church in community which is connected and networked with both other communities within all nations and with the Catholic tradition and Church. No community can exist in isolation from either. No community is complete in itself. But each community is church. In all communities the church is collegial, collaborative, team ministry and servant leadership.

V II. Conclusion

This statement is very much a work in process. It remains open to future dialogue and invites others to participation. In this incompleteness, it reflects the very communities whose experiences were considered. These are small Christian communities whose lives remain open to further dialogue and invite others to participation. They are church, ever becoming and ever inviting all into further communion, further life with the Risen Christ.

FURTHER REFLECTIONS ON THE CHRISTOLOGY AND ECCLESIOLOGY OF SMALL ECCLESIAL COMMUNITIES

Sixto J. Garcia

These reflections are meant to be a meditation on small Christian communities, submitted as a contribution to the Theological Consultation on Small Christian Communities, celebrated at the University of Notre Dame, October 20–24, 1996. I will draw from my own experience with and within small Christian communities as they celebrate and minister in South Florida and, more specifically, within the Diocese of Palm Beach. I choose to keep this concrete experience of SCCs in my diocese as my constant source of theological qualification and critique, since I feel that general theological reflections always need specific historical grounding to be true and vitally authentic.

I should make clear that I was not present at the consultation. Although I have carefully read the very insightful papers presented at that time, I did not participate in the dynamics of dialogue. This means, in a sense, that my mode of interpretation of these documents lacks the concrete, personal engagement or "belonging-ness" to the process of discussion that Hans-Georg Gadamer feels is essential to listen to a text. I trust that my own experiences with Hispanic SCCs and my own Christological reflections will allow me to listen to the consultation papers and their vital horizon humbly and adequately and to dialogue with them in a theologically responsible fashion.

I propose to look at three particular aspects of the SCCs: First, I would like to meditate on the role of the trained theologian active within the SCCs. Second, I intend to look at the SCCs as the privileged place for a fully experienced kenotic Christology. Third, I will attempt to argue that the kenotic identity of the SCCs will challenge the present and future Church to be a kenotic Church—more than that, it will summon the Church to realize that she can only be Church as kenotic, suffering, servant Church.

The Function of the Theologian within SCCs: Prophet and Poet

We need to address the present and future role of the trained theologian within the SCCs, if for no other reason than that, more often than not, it is the theologian who writes and speaks about the small ecclesial communities, makes their importance known, and eventually mediates the theological understanding of their presence and activity. The Notre Dame Consultation papers reflect this reality. A more selfish reason why I wish to address this issue is that I teach Systematics at St. Vincent de Paul Regional Seminary and serve as teacher and facilitator of formation within Hispanic SCCs and have often struggled to make sense of the correlation between these two different missions.

I have been involved within the Hispanic SCCs in my diocese almost exclusively as a teacher and facilitator. This is always a dangerous situation, since the delusions and temptations of power and arrogance can easily emerge. The practices of these communities have proven to be uniquely enriching experiences where such temptations have been arrested from the start. I have discovered the power of vulnerable, kenotic, loving service active within these groups, and I dare say I have grown in the unique and unsettling realization that, as my teaching unfolded, their own concrete experience of Jesus Christ was already a source of grace for me, summoning me to conversion. It did not take long for me to realize that they were teaching me in the most ample sense of the word, that is, teaching from within the bowels of their experience, their prayer and worship, and their vulnerable and freely-given service. My academic theology was challenged by their praxis, by their lived Christology and ecclesiology; I found my book-learned theology wanting and realized that I needed to rethink all of it in light of the real, concrete experience of my SCC. I am called to appropiate this ongoing encounter of theory with praxis within my mind and heart. This, I am deeply convinced, is the future of theology in and for the Church: a reflection from within the heart of SCCs' worship, of powerlessness and vulnerability, of healing and transforming love.

This theology truly born of the experience of the people, however, can be genuine, only if the theologian becomes broken with the broken, powerless with the powerless, only if he or she enters their world and becomes a suffering servant with them. Monika Hellwig's respectful and delicate critique of Eurocentric academic theology is a good reminder of the call we have to demythologize theological systems begotten within the ivory towers of isolated Academia, within computer-heavy rooms quite remote from the mud, dirt, blood, and tears of the people of God.

Our community is very heterogeneous: mostly Mexicans and Guatemalans, Dominicans, a generous sprinkling of Puerto Ricans, Salvadoreans, and a few Cubans. In any other situation and place in South Florida, this diversity would inevitably result in serious cultural friction. But in our group there seems to be a realization that, besides a common ancestral language—Spanish—and a common social situation—struggling to survive, often facing discrimination—our faith and liturgical involvement is the strongest common ground of friendship and solidarity. This is, indeed, a place where the chemistry of Christian love really happens: God's love becomes truly present because community members love one another the only way that love can be experienced, that is, from a vulnerable, letting-go decision that frees the beloved. Intercultural frictions are infrequent, because there is an overarching acceptance of Jesus Christ's healing compassion present in our midst.

I propose to define the role of the theologian within the SCCs as that of a poet and prophet. The theologian is called to be the poet who expresses the intimate life of the community through the metaphors and symbols that articulate, much more deeply than descriptive language, the horizon of faith of the men and women who suffer and pray every day. Following upon Paul Ricoeur's notion of symbol, the theologian/poet must allow the symbols—the community's rather than his own—to unveil new meaning, new being, to disclose a radically new world of paradox, the Christian paradox, where total brokenness and radical powerlessness become the privileged place for grace, for transforming love, healing nearness, and forgiving intimacy.

Theological reflection within the small community also involves the dangerous calling to prophecy. The theologian is called to help the community disclose the prophetic core of its symbols. Here again the theologian recognizes that his role as a prophet is not one of power or authority over the community but rather one of serving the already existing prophetic profile of the group as a whole.

Given the situation of oppresion that many SCCs experience, it is not very difficult to see that the very commitment to a true and empowering kenotic practice already constitutes a clearly powerful denunciation of existing oppression. My experience with both my communities witnessess to this reality. The decision to live the life of abandonment and powerlessness, understood as a letting-go of manipulation, in order to practice a prophetic mission within our local Church already raises a clamor against the manipulative and consumeristic lifestyle of surrounding society. To take this a step further, these communities' lifestyle is in strong contrast to the lifestyle of those Catholics who flock to wealthy parishes, who organize gala fund-raising dinners in plush, exclusive local country clubs and hotels, and who seem to ignore the faith communities that live in the social and economic periphery of both Church and society.

The SCCs as a Privileged Place for a Kenotic Christology

French philosopher Maurice Blondel, whose thought was so uniquely influential for many important Catholic theologians of the conciliar and post-conciliar period (Karl Rahner, Henri Bouillard, Henri de Lubac, just to mention a few), offered an alternative to the extrinsic approach to apologetics and theology proper to the Neo-Scholastic method. Blondel looked at the concrete form of human action, unfolding in a tension between the two modes of the will: the willing will—that is, the will always going beyond categorical, concrete acts—and the willed will that expresses our inner dynamism toward God incompletely and deficiently. Given the on-going movement of human volition, static propositions and doctrines and historically decontextualized proofs cannot allow us to properly understand God and the Christian tradition. Truth, argued Blondel, particularly truth expressed in tradition, can only be encountered in full and experienced as true within a personal, committed engagement of the human person with the tradition, that is, within the context of human praxis, of human doing, not merely theorizing.

Taking Blondel's philosophy of human action and personal commitment as a starting point, I wish to argue that the experienced and contemplated profile of Jesus Christ, that is, Christology and especially the Christology of the future Church, can only be found within the personal, vulnerably committed relationship of a Christian community with the Crucified and Risen One. This allows us to reflect on kenotic Christology, the Christology of the broken, powerless, and self-emptying Christ, from the concrete, lived experience of small faith communities.

Many Hispanic groups in my area—most of them—function in situations of kenosis. As I mentioned above, many suffer overt or subtle discrimination, not infrequently at the hands of fellow Hispanics whose more affluent social situation grants them entrance into the world of the power parishes, country clubs, and hotels. The situation of Hispanic groups in the western part of Palm Beach County, where most members of the large Hispanic community are manual laborers, sugar cane cutters, or rural farmers, is particularly difficult. In most cases, their parishes are the only source of help or support. Their wages are meager and they often work around the clock, with little or no rest. The local law-enforcement authorities generally support the repressive structures and tend to be particularly harsh with Hispanic residents of scant economic means and outside the range of appropiate legal representation.

The kenotic experience of these communities is a living cry of prophetic anguish aimed at the traditions of lying, manipulation, controlling, and oppression that society and the structural Church exhibit. The Church's participation in institutional violence takes place as pastors and wealthy lay leaders choose to ignore the objective structures of mortal sin within their own local churches and instead embrace the ways of the oppressor: power struggles, manipulation, low wages, discrimination. This presents a very scandalous situation for many who see the Church not as participants but at a distance. There are those who ponder the following paradox: on the one hand, a powerful tradition of social justice documents going back one hundred and six years; on the other hand, practical disregard for, and even contradiction of these social justice norms shown by pastors and affluent laity.

The committed Christian living her or his commitment within the SCCs realizes that only a personal engagement with the Crucified Jesus can bring about a just healing of these unjust situations. He or she may become aware that Christology can be developed, at a primary level of language, only by praxis and contemplation, and only at a secondary level by actual "theologizing." Only life and mission issuing forth from a personal commitment with the radical brokenness of the Cross can function as reforming and renewing prophecy—not just a prophecy that points away from the prophet to a distant place, but a prophecy that is already in the process of being fulfilled by the prophet him or herself.

Catherine Nearny's insightful paper stresses the need to celebrate Word and Sacrament as a privileged context for mission (and hence, for prophecy). I submit that the SCCs' eucharistic celebrations must always be mindful of the deeper symbol of broken bread and spilt wine—a reminder of the dangerous memory of the broken Jesus, whose love takes on the ultimate risk—humiliating, crushing, seemingly anhilating death. This is the risk the Church is called to take but not very often does: total surrender and vulnerability for the sake of the poor, the discriminated, the oppressed, the homeless. I have to assume this is what Vatican II had in mind when it referred to the Church as sacrament—a sacrament of hope, of compassion, of insane love for the others, the same insanity, madness, folly of God that Paul sings about in I Corinthians 1:25: an insane love always stronger than the pretended wisdom of men and women who live the "correct" religion, who attend the "correct" parishes. A Church that is not looked upon with dread and suspicion by the

powers of evil, of oppression, is a dysfunctional Church, a compla-
cent Church, ultimately, a betraying Church.

Finally, I would like to offer one more Christological point. The
Basque theologian Xavier Picaza has argued that the death—the
"assasination" as he chooses to call it—of Jesus, a violent death
brought about by a violent, manipulative, arrogantly selfish religious
and political structure, gathers all the violence, injustice, death, and
suffering of the world in one single moment of self-renouncing love.
I tell my students that we may accept the ancient wisdom of the
Church concerning the Cross: Christ suffered the most because he
loved the most. He was, is the sacrament of God's ineffable over-
flowing reality of love. In the Cross, Jesus took upon himself the
cry of all the suffering, oppressed, and despised of the world, took
it and affirmed it, in one moment of total self-surrender, of total
risk-taking, of total desolation. And upon gathering the cry of the
suffering within his love, within his broken heart, he created a para-
doxical void of self wherein grace came rushing, streaming in to fill
the void—Resurrection. The Cross of Jesus, therefore, stands as
the ultimate prophetic utterance, as the ultimate memory of God's
love, always affirming, always transforming, always unspeakably dangerous.

The SCCs as Sacraments in the Becoming of the Future Kenotic Church

Our preceding remarks bring us to the question of the SCCs'
role in the future Church. The importance of this question is borne
by the fact that the Church of the future is already happening. The
SCCs are unfolding as a proto-sacramental symbol of that Church;
this is true at least within my ecclesial area. As the next millennium
slides in upon us, smaller communities seem more and more attractive to those men and women within the people of God struggling
with social and institutional violence, with unjust economic and political structures, with foundational meaninglessness in their lives as
the "larger" Church seemingly turn a deaf ear on these concerns. I
have seldom read local pastoral documents focusing on the concrete
issues of injustice suffered by Hispanic communities in the area. All

of these factors emphasize the appeal of living, committed, wor-shipping, and prophetically missionary small Christian communi-ties.

This will not be an easy process. The small SCCs will always be signs of contradiction to the powerful in the Church. The SCCs refuse to be manipulated, to be controlled, to be forced to fit into the narrow gage of the consumeristic, manipulating Church. They seem to have a life of their own, and indeed they do. This is the life of the Spirit. The Spirit promised, announced by Jesus to his own (John 14:26; 15:26), unleashed at the moment of his death (John 19:30), and breathed upon the community by the Risen Lord (John 20:22), remains active in the Church of the crucified, remains the life-giving Spirit in the lives of the threatened and oppressed. The Spirit is the affirmation and promise that God continues to offer to God's people through the death and Resurrection of Jesus. The privileged place for the activity of the Crucified and Risen Jesus today is within the small communities, the kenotic and prophetic communities that unfold unceasingly as sacraments of the future kenotic Church.

Select Bibliography

Blondel, Maurice. *Action* (1893). Trans. Oliva Blanchette. Notre Dame, Ind.: University of Notre Dame Press, 1984.

——. *The Letter on Apologetics and History and Dogma.* Trans. Alexander Dru and Illtyd Trethowan. Grand Rapids, Mich.: Eerdmans, 1994.

Flannery, Austin, ed. *Vatican Council II.* Vol. 1: *The Conciliar and Postconsiliar Documents.* Northport, N.Y. / Dublin, Ireland: Costello / Dominican, 1996.

Gutierrez, Gustavo. *Beber en su propio pozo.* Salamanca: Sigueme, 1986.

——. *Hablar de Dios desde el sufrimiento del inocente.* Salamanca: Sigueme, 1986.

Richard Lucien. *Christ: The Self-Emptying of God.* New York / Mahwah, N.J.: Paulist Press, 1997.

AFTERWORD

Toward the Church of the Twenty-First Century

Carol Frances Jegen, B.V.M.

Notre Dame's recent meetings on small Christian communities call for theological reflection regarding the Church of the future. Some of the pertinent insights are mentioned here briefly as an invitation for further theological development.

Reflecting on the worldwide phenomenon of these small faith communities highlights the action of the Holy Spirit in the era of Vatican II, this time of New Pentecost as designated by John XXIII. In many ways the global emergence of these communities parallels the growth of the Church described in Acts, that New Testament book of remarkable witness to the Holy Spirit's action in the First Pentecost event.

As genuine Christian faith communities, these gatherings witness to the need for sharing concerns, hopes, and challenges. Such open, trusting sharing in faith is necessary for the vitality of each small Christian community in each and every culture. In this process a growing awareness of the presence of the risen Jesus gives the needed strength and joy in continuing the mission of Jesus in the manifold circumstances of our times. As true "followers of Christ" small Christian community members identify with and respond to "the joys and the hopes, the griefs and the anxieties of the people of this age, especially those who are poor or in any way afflicted" (*Gaudium et Spes* 1). Small Christian communities witness to authentic "Church in the Modern World." They are needed leaven for the Church of the future.

A century ago Cardinal Newman alerted us to the necessity of "consulting the faithful" in regard to the Church's response to the

questions and concerns of people in any period of history. What
potential there is in the faith-sharing experience of small Christian
communities for the needed development of doctrine in the Church
of the coming century. New structures need to be developed for
such dialogue to take place.

One of the most significant factors of the second and third gatherings at Notre Dame (1990 and 1991) was the international participation. Persons from Asia, Africa, Latin America, Europe, and
North America experienced different cultural expressions of the
contemporary Church. The genuine respect and appreciation of
each community's experience and orientation witnessed to a unity
that cherished diversity. Those two international meetings were mi-
crocosms of a Church that is truly catholic in its global outreach.
What a powerful witness to a world violently torn by ethnic and
national rivalries!

Small Christian communities give hope to the ecumenical movement. The SCC witness to smaller gatherings of Christians who are
related to and united with the whole Church resonates with those
concerns of Orthodox and Protestant Christians who seek for ways
of unity that respect the vitality and contributions of different community identities in the universal Church. The global SCC presence
may well be one of the Holy Spirit's responses to the Church's ongoing prayer for Christian unity.

The final decade of the twentieth century has seen a growing
interest in Trinitarian theology. There is a yearning for a pastoral
theology of Trinitarian life, one that helps faithful Christians grow
in the realization of the wondrous divine life they possess along with
some understanding of the power of that divine life for community
living. The characteristic ways of mutuality and inclusion in the SCC
faith-sharing process is one more witness of God's Trinitarian presence within and among us. In small Christian communities there is
an experience of community life that can provide a necessary and
viable grounding for the pastoral Trinitarian theology so needed in
the Church today.

In John's Gospel, Jesus told us how his followers would be known.
"This is how all will know you for my disciples: your love for one

another" (Jn 13:35). All through the centuries of Christian presence, the authentic sign of that presence was love, a love that responded to human need whatever it might be. The heart of small Christian community life is the members' love for one another. Such witness of genuine love is our basic hope for the Church of the twenty-first century.

APPENDIX
Participants

Rev. Art Baranowski
Director, National Alliance of
    Parishes
Restructuring into Communities
Marysville, Mich.

Margaret Bisgrove
Bonita Springs, Fla.

Rosemary Bleuher
Director of Adult Education/SCC
    Formation
Diocese of Joliet
Joliet, Ill.

Mrs. Alicia Butkiewicz
Cochabama, Bolivia

Rev. Curt Cadorette, M.M.
University of Rochester
Rochester, N.Y.

Carolee Chanona
Belize, Central America

Donna Ciangio, O.P.
National Pastoral Life Center
New York, N.Y.

Rev. Michael E. Connors, C.S.C.
Fatima Retreat House
Notre Dame, Ind.

William D'Antonio
Washington, D.C.

Most Rev. Joseph Remi DeRoo
Diocese of Victoria
Victoria, B.C., Canada

Peter Eichten
Minneapolis, Minn.

David Fajardo
Coachella, Calif.

Rev. Daniel Groody, C.S.C.
Holy Cross Center
Berkeley, Calif.

Edni M. L. Gugelmin
São Paulo, Brazil

Rev. Joseph G. Healey, M.M.
Dar es Salaam, Tanzania
East Africa

Kevin Healy
Inter-American Foundation
Washington, D.C.

Monika Hellwig, Executive Director
Association of Catholic Colleges and
    Universities
Washington, D.C.

Mary Ann Hinsdale, I.H.M.
College of the Holy Cross
Worcester, Mass.

Barbara Howard
Arvada, Colo.

Most Rev. William A. Hughes, D.D.
Retired Bishop of Covington
Covington, Ky.

Carol Frances Jegen, B.V.M.
Loyola University Institute of
    Pastoral Studies
Chicago, Ill.

Crescentia John
Bombay, India

Susan Lautenbach
Naperville, Ill.

Rev. Bernard Lee, S.M.
Loyola University, New Orleans
New Orleans, La.

Helen M. Lewis
New Market, Tenn.

Most Rev. James W. Malone, D.D.
Retired Bishop of Youngstown
Youngstown, Ohio

Rev. José Marins
Brazil

Mary Clare McCabe
South Bend, Ind.

Rev. William D. McCarthy, M.M.
Center for Mission Research and
   Study
Maryknoll, N.Y.

Rose Musimba
Nairobi, Kenya

Archbishop Raphael Ndingi
   Mawana'a Nzeki
Bishop of Nairobi
Nairobi, Kenya, East Africa

Catherine T. Nerney, S.S.J.
Chestnut Hill College
Philadelphia, Pa.

Robert Thomas O'Gorman
Institute of Pastoral Studies
Loyola University, Chicago
Chicago, Ill.

Rev. Paul Philibert, O.P.
Director of the Institute for Church
   Life
Notre Dame, Ind.

Anne Reissner
Center for Mission Research and
   Study
Maryknoll, N.Y.

Jane Elyse Russell, O.S.F.
Milwaukee, Wis.

Rev. Aylward Shorter, M.Afr.,
   Principal
Tangaza College
The Catholic University of Eastern
   Africa
Nairobi, Kenya

Sally Sommers
Villa Park, Ill.

Teolide Maria Trevisan
Brazil

Terry A. Veling
Catholic Theological Union
Australia

Rev. Dr. John Mary Waliggo
Uganda Catholic Secretariat
Uganda

Robert H. Wheeler
Naperville, Ill.

Victoria Yuk-lin Yeung
Catholic Diocese Centre
Hong Kong